Social and Emotional Learning for Advanced Children in Early Childhood

This book illuminates the complexities of social and emotional learning (SEL) during early childhood and provides readers with supportive tools to enhance and advance social and emotional skills among young children within their homes and classrooms.

Affective development is critical to childhood development – this guide gives parents and educators concrete strategies to support students' social skills, relationship development, and positive mental health. Expertly blending theory with practice, *Social and Emotional Learning for Advanced Children in Early Childhood: Birth to 8* presents vital background information, real-life examples, diverse case studies, discussion questions, and action steps for implementing SEL into any early childhood environment.

By including both what is understood about social and emotional development in early childhood as well as the proven methods and approaches for working with young children, this comprehensive guide is a must read for all adults striving to make a positive impact in early childhood development.

Bronwyn MacFarlane, Ph.D., is Professor at Arkansas State University. She has diverse experiences teaching gifted students, leading educational programs, designing, reviewing, evaluating, and implementing differentiated early childhood curriculum for advanced learners, as well as providing inspirational professional talks for teachers, administrators, parents, and students.

Ellen Honeck, Ph.D., is Assistant Head of School at Tessellations School in Cupertino, CA. She has been involved in the field of gifted education for over 20 years in various roles including classroom teacher, gifted specialist, administrator, adjunct professor, and Associate Director of a Gifted Education Institute. She also consults with private and public schools and districts across the United States.

Social and Emotional Learning for Advanced Children in Early Childhood

Birth to 8

Bronwyn MacFarlane and Ellen Honeck

NEW YORK AND LONDON

Designed cover image: Top left © Getty Images. Bottom left: © Jose Luis Pelaez Inc / Getty Images. Right: Bronwyn MacFarlane.

First published 2023
by Routledge
605 Third Avenue, New York, NY 10158

and by Routledge
4 Park Square, Milton Park, Abingdon, Oxon, OX14 4RN

Routledge is an imprint of the Taylor & Francis Group, an informa business

© 2023 Taylor & Francis

The right of Bronwyn MacFarlane and Ellen Honeck to be identified as authors of this work has been asserted in accordance with sections 77 and 78 of the Copyright, Designs and Patents Act 1988.

All rights reserved. No part of this book may be reprinted or reproduced or utilised in any form or by any electronic, mechanical, or other means, now known or hereafter invented, including photocopying and recording, or in any information storage or retrieval system, without permission in writing from the publishers.

Trademark notice: Product or corporate names may be trademarks or registered trademarks, and are used only for identification and explanation without intent to infringe.

ISBN: 978-1-032-40570-4 (hbk)
ISBN: 978-1-032-40571-1 (pbk)
ISBN: 978-1-003-35369-0 (ebk)

DOI: 10.4324/9781003353690

Typeset in Palatino
by Deanta Global Publishing Services, Chennai, India

In honor of my son, Clark Ted Brian; my husband, Greg;
and my mother, Beverly,
who provide daily lessons about gentle parenting
and teaching.
– Bronwyn MacFarlane

Dedicated to my husband, Cole; children, Haley and AJ,
for their continued support and encouragement; and in
memory of my friend and mentor, Shannon B. Jones.
– Ellen Honeck

Contents

List of Tables viii
Preface ix
About the Authors x

1 Understanding Social and Emotional Learning in
   Early Childhood: Introductions and Definitions 1

2 Overview of Social Emotional Learning in
   Early Childhood 17

3 Characteristics and Case Studies of Very Young
   Children, Birth to Two Years 38

4 Characteristics and Case Studies of Preschool
   Children, Ages Three To Five Years 61

5 Characteristics and Case Studies of School-Age
   Children, Ages Six to Eight Years 76

6 Conclusion 91

Appendix A: Book and Article Resources 101
Appendix B: Social and Emotional Learning Curriculum
Resources 109
Appendix C: Organizational Resources 114
Appendix D: Definitions of Relevant Terminology 116

List of Tables

1.1	Developmental Trends (McDevitt & Ormrod, 2013, pp. 26–27)	4
1.2	Fast Facts about Early Childhood Development	5
1.3	Possible Characteristics of Advanced Development	7
2.1	Social and Emotional Learning Strategies	34
3.1	Social Emotional Milestones for Birth to Two Years	41
3.2	Case Analysis for Zachary	50
3.3	Case Analysis for Sylvia	53
3.4	Toys and Activities Appropriate for Birth to Two Years of Age	54
3.5	Summary of Case Analyses Needs and Suggestions: Very Young Children, Birth to Two Years	59
4.1	From Table 1.1: Developmental Trends between Ages Three and Five Years	62
4.2	Summary of Case Analyses Needs and Suggestions: Preschool Children, Ages Three to Five Years	74
5.1	From Table 1.1: Developmental Trends between Ages Six and Eight Years (McDevitt & Ormrod, 2013, pp. 26–27)	77
5.2	Affective Characteristics of Giftedness (Clark, 2013)	78
5.3	Areas of Giftedness Identification	80
5.4	Summary of Case Analyses Needs and Suggestions: School-Age Children, Ages Six to Eight Years	89

Preface

Thank you for sharing our interest in this important topic about social and emotional learning in early childhood with advanced children. This book provides valuable information and guidance to understand the complexities associated with social and emotional learning that occurs during the stages of early childhood, with a focus on how to develop these skills, a grounding based in research, and is practically designed to provide specific strategies to help children.

This book came about when the authors began collaborating as volunteer network leaders in the National Association for Gifted Children (NAGC) for the early childhood and counseling networks. With a combined 50 years of experience in education across a variety of roles, the authors recognized the importance of sharing these ideas about psychosocial development with educators and parents working with young children. We believe that this book is a much-needed publication for readers interested in social and emotional development, early childhood, gifted education, and meeting the needs of these children. By increasing attention to healthy social and emotional growth, advanced children will be more likely to experience differentiated learning experiences appropriate to their unique needs.

This book is important because it provides a friendly resource for adults with young children about how to help develop their awareness of their own self and others' needs for social interaction that is kind, gentle, and understanding of one another. To build empathy through early life learning experiences, adults can strategically consider and apply the positive social emotional learning techniques provided as well as the thoughtful prompts for collegial discussion. This resource should be used by and shared among families, educators, and caregivers across settings from homes to educational programs and school settings.

About the Authors

Bronwyn MacFarlane, Ph.D., has experience evaluating programming, inspiring educators, and providing professional workshops. She was Professor of Gifted Education at the University of Arkansas at Little Rock for 13 years prior to joining the doctoral faculty at Arkansas State University. Named one of the Top 3 Professors at the University of Arkansas at Little Rock in 2021 by the Board of Visitors with the Faculty Excellence Award for Service, Bronwyn's service has been recognized at the university, state, and national levels with the 2018 NAGC Early Leader Award for exemplary work in the professional field of gifted education and with the Arkansas gifted educator and Challenger state awards. She was elected to serve on the seven-member Executive Committee of the World Council for Gifted and Talented Children as the member from the United States. She also received the 2020 College Faculty Excellence Award in Research and Creative Endeavors for producing over 13 publications in one year. Dr. MacFarlane published five books including *Social and Emotional Learning for Advanced Children in Early Childhood: Birth to 8* (2023 with Ellen Honeck); *Specialized Schools for High-Ability Learners: Designing and Implementing Programs in Specialized School Settings* (2018); *Second Language Learning for the Gifted: Connection and Communication for the 21st Century* (2017 with Joyce VanTassel-Baska & Ariel Baska); *STEM Education for High-Ability Learners: Designing and Implementing Programming* (2016); *Leading Change in Gifted Education: The Festschrift of Dr. Joyce VanTassel-Baska* (2009 with Tamra Stambaugh); numerous articles, 25 book chapters; has delivered over 150 presentations; and taught 35 university graduate course topics. Leadership roles have included College Associate Dean; Academic Dean of the Summer Institute for Gifted at Princeton; service as NAGC Past-Chair of the STEM Network and the Counseling & Guidance Network; Guest Editor for *Roeper Review* and for *Frontiers in Education: Leadership in Education*; and national columnist of "The Curriculum Corner" for *Teaching for High Potential* magazine. With four degrees earned from the College of William and Mary, Stephens College, and the University of Missouri, she has served as reviewer of grants, journal manuscripts, and conference proposals. As an educational leader, Dr. MacFarlane is regularly invited to speak to audiences about talent development, perseverance around barriers, and improving organizational/program design and culture. She enjoys family time with her handsome husband, her talented toddler, and her effervescent mother together storytelling, playing outdoors, gardening, reading, dinner parties, music, and dancing.

Ellen Honeck, Ph.D., is currently the Assistant Head of School at Tessellations: The Beneventi School in Cupertino, California. She previously worked as the Director of Curriculum and Instruction at The Knox School of Santa Barbara, Gifted and Talented Department Manager in Denver Public Schools, and with various online, private, and public schools. Dr. Honeck has been involved in the field of gifted education working in various roles as a classroom teacher, administrator, gifted specialist, curriculum developer, consultant, adjunct professor, and Associate Director. She has contributed to NAGC in several roles including an At-Large Board member, past network chair and chair-elect and a member of the Whole Child Task Force. She received the 2021 Professional Development Network Award for "Culturally Responsive Gifted Education" and the 2016 NAGC President's Award. Dr. Honeck co-authored *Social and Emotional Learning for Advanced Children in Early Childhood: Birth to 8* (2023 with Bronwyn MacFarlane), *Teaching Gifted Children in Today's Preschool and Primary Classrooms, Let's Play!, Around my House!,* and *Let's Go to the Market!,* all part of the "Smart Start Series," *Teacher Compendium for Human Rights Education,* and several chapters, curriculum units, and articles. Dr. Honeck is a frequent presenter at national, international, state, and local conferences as well as consulting with various schools and school districts across the United States. Her professional passions in gifted education include culturally responsive gifted education, early childhood, instructional strategies, questioning, creativity, and curriculums for advanced learners. Personally, she enjoys spending time with her husband, daughter, and son. She is passionate about ALL things Disney including traveling to the parks, learning about the behind-the-scenes of movies and parks, and is also an avid Denver Bronco Football Fan.

1

Understanding Social and Emotional Learning in Early Childhood

Introductions and Definitions

We have daily routines as adults in which we interact with a variety of people both inside and outside of our homes. In each of these settings, as we move from home to school to work to community throughout our week, our interactions with others impact our social and emotional well-being. We influence others as they influence us in return. When we recognize and understand the impact that we have upon each other, we are better able to react, respond, and successfully navigate the challenges that we face. Understanding our social interactions, personal mindset, self-understanding, and awareness is critical to each of us throughout our lifetime. Children develop a personal view of themselves based on their interactions with adults. Educators, parents, and families play a key role in shaping and contributing to a child's sense of self. As authors, our goal with this book is to provide adults with a discussion of the tools they can use to help young children develop positive and healthy interactions with themselves and with others. Social and emotional understanding may be the most important factor when determining a child's future success, and understanding the critical role of how adults

DOI: 10.4324/9781003353690-1

can impact and guide a child's individual outlook is the focus of the following chapters.

This book provides valuable information and guidance to understand the complexities associated with social and emotional learning that occurs during the stages of early childhood with a focus on how to develop these skills. We have written this book with a grounding based in research designed to provide specific strategies to help children and translated to practical use with children (Neihart, Pfeiffer, & Cross, 2016; Cohen et al., 2005). Our social emotional interactions and processes include both intra- (internal to self) and inter- (external to others) personal processes. As we discuss social emotional development and strategies, we will focus on an individual's experience, expression, and management of emotions and the ability to establish positive and rewarding relationships with others.

Background on Social Emotional Learning

The National Association for the Education of Young Children (NAEYC) recognizes that social emotional learning (SEL) is important for its role in increasing the achievement of all children and reducing learning gaps. NAEYC provides guidelines for developmentally appropriate practice to promote the learning and development of young children. These five guidelines include (1) creating a caring community of learners, (2) teaching to enhance development and learning, (3) planning a curriculum to achieve important goals, (4) assessing children's development and learning, and (5) establishing reciprocal relationships with families (NAEYC, 2009). These guidelines are important to environments that interact with young children to enhance their development and skills for learning.

Developmental Stages and Characteristics (Birth to Age Eight)

In this book, we focus on early childhood as defined by the National Association for the Education of Young Children (NAEYC) ranging from birth through age eight. The level of development is different at each age level as are the characteristics across physical, cognitive, and social emotional domains. Specific chapters will focus on the differences at each age level, birth to two years, three to five years, and six- to eight-year-olds.

From birth to two years, children's physical development includes motor skills such as rolling over, sitting up, crawling, standing, walking ability, to reach and grab; rapid growth and weight gain; development of self-help skills (eating, drinking, toilet training, washing); and ability to coordinate vision with the small muscles of the hands. Cognitive development among babies and infants includes learning to distinguish among different faces, the ability to imitate simple gestures, and the ability to remember people and objects out of sight. There is rapid growth in early communication including crying, gestures, facial expressions, one-word and multiple-word sentences, as well as development of cause and effect relationships. Social and emotional development among babies and infants involves the formation of close bonds with caregivers, the use of words to name needs and desires, side-by-side play with peers, awareness of ownership and boundaries of self, and developing a sense of power and will.

During the toddler years from ages three to five, physical development includes increased motor skills such as running, skipping, throwing, building; increased competence in basic self-care; more mature looking physical features; acquisition of fine motor skills – pencil grip; and transition away from afternoon nap. Meanwhile, cognitive development from three to five years centers upon dramatic play and fantasy with peers, ability to draw simple figures, acknowledging colors, letters, and numbers, recognition and retelling of familiar stories and events, reasoning that is often illogical, frequent self-talk, and limited understanding of how adults typically interpret events. Social and emotional development for the toddler includes developing understanding of gender and ethnicity, development of the ability to defer immediate gratification – sharing, modest appreciation that other people have their own desires, and some demonstration of sympathy for people in distress.

Physical development for the *six- to eight-year-old child* focuses on successful imitations of complex physical movements, such

TABLE 1.1 Developmental Trends (McDevitt & Ormrod, 2013, pp. 26–27)

Stages	Physical Development	Cognitive Development	Social Emotional Development
Birth to Two Years	• Motor skills including rolling over, sitting up, crawling, standing, walking • Ability to reach and grab • Rapid growth and weight gain • Development of self-help skills (eating, drinking, toilet training, washing) • Ability to coordinate vision with small muscles of hands	• Distinguish among various faces • Rapid growth in communication including crying, gestures, facial expressions, one-word and multiple-word sentences • Ability to imitate simple gestures • Ability to remember people and objects out of sight • Development of cause and effect relationships	• Formation of close bonds with caregivers • Use of words to name needs and desires • Side-by-side play with peers • Awareness of ownership and boundaries of self • Developing sense of power and will
Three to Five years	• Increased motor skills such as running, skipping, throwing, building • Increased competence in basic self-care • More mature looking physical features • Acquisition of fine motor skills – pencil grip • Transition away from afternoon nap	• Dramatic play and fantasy with peers • Ability to draw simple figures • Acknowledge colors, letters, and numbers • Recognition and retelling of familiar stories and events • Reasoning that is often illogical • Frequent self-talk • Limited understanding of how adults typically interpret events	• Developing understanding of gender and ethnicity • Development of the ability to defer immediate gratification – sharing • Modest appreciation that other people have their own desires • Some demonstration of sympathy for people in distress
Six to Eight Years	• Successful imitations of complex physical movements – ability to ride a bicycle • Participation in organized sports • Steady gains in height and weight • Refinement of gross motor skills • Loss and replacement of primary teeth	• Development of basic skills in reading, writing, math, and other academic subject areas • Ability to reason logically about concrete objects and events in the immediate environment	• Increasing awareness of how one's own abilities compare with peers • Desire for time with age-mates • Increasing ability to have responsibilities such as chores • Adherence to rules of games • Understanding of basic moral principles (fairness and equity)

McDevitt, T.M. & Ormrod, J.E., (2013). *Child development and education (fifth edition).* Pearson.

as the ability to ride a bicycle, participation in organized sports, steady gains in height and weight, refinement of gross motor skills, and the loss and replacement of primary teeth. Cognitive development for the six- to eight-year-old child includes the development of basic skills in reading, writing, math, and other academic subject areas as well as the ability to reason logically about concrete objects and events in the immediate environment.

As children move through the early developmental stages, skills continue to build upon one another, and advanced characteristics may begin to be revealed in addition to normal development. Some advanced children may progress through the developmental stages and acquire skills at a faster pace than the average student.

TABLE 1.2 Fast Facts about Early Childhood Development

Consider the following understandings about early childhood:

1. Fifty percent of intelligence among all children is formed by age four
2. A child's most productive and influential years of learning occur before the age of five
3. In general, a person's brain reaches 95 percent of its maximum size by age six
4. From birth, babies sense and react to their parents' moods, such as being angry or sad
5. Babies as young as six months can experience a range of feelings, including sadness and fear, but 69 percent of parents think this developmental milestone occurs later in their life
6. Routines make young children feel safe and secure
7. If a child is sensitive and reactive to sensory experiences, parents can avoid situations that overstimulate sensitivities and cause discomfort
8. Children are capable of feeling good about themselves and the early roots of their emerging self-esteem occurs between ages one and two. While 43 percent of parents think that a child is capable of such feelings by age two, the majority of them (53 percent) do not think a child can experience these feelings until they are older (National Center for Infants, Toddlers, and Families, 2009)

Advanced, High Ability, and Gifted Children

While definitions of giftedness vary, there are some common characteristics among advanced and gifted children. Not all characteristics are present with every child and other factors (such as economic status, cultural background, ethnic background) may influence the way characteristics may be displayed. Let's take a look at the characteristics of advanced young children.

Characteristics of Young Gifted Children

Understanding child development and growth is important for parents and caregivers in order to recognize advanced or delayed abilities. Recognition and understanding is critical to help continue a child's growth in a positive way. Young gifted children usually show their special abilities before entering elementary school (Lim, 2009). At preschool, they may exhibit advanced understanding or performance in one or a variety of areas. There are many signs of giftedness. Parents and preschool teachers should take note when some of the earliest signs of giftedness emerge consistently.

The following characteristics of giftedness do not all need to be present for a young child to be gifted (Silverman, 1993; Clark, 2013). These characteristics merge with the child's developmental level. As each child is different, a particular advanced child might exhibit some or all of the characteristics and developmental trends listed in Table 1.3.

While research varies as to the degree or level in which the specific gifted characteristics interact, "gifted learners show characteristics different from their age peers in each of the areas of functioning, although all gifted individuals have their own unique patterns of characteristics and no gifted learner exhibits every characteristic in every area" (Clark, 1992, p. 37). Young children who are advanced in their development are talented, regardless of the specific developmental area of physical, cognitive, or affective. And, some advanced children may demonstrate advanced behaviors across several of these areas. Verbally talented children speak in sentences earlier than children of the same age and often use higher-level vocabulary. Mathematically talented children acquire counting skills and number concepts sooner than their peers. Musically talented children may sing on key, demonstrate an interest in musical instruments, and stop what they are doing to listen to music. Artistic children demonstrate artwork that is similar to products created by older children. Kinesthetically or psychomotor-talented children demonstrate advanced movement skills. Spatially talented children often are

TABLE 1.3 Possible Characteristics of Advanced Development

Physical Development	Cognitive Development	Affective Development
• Unusual alertness in infancy • Less need for sleep in infancy • Long attention span and intense concentration • High activity level • Smiling or recognizing caretakers early • Intense reactions to noise, pain, frustration • Unusual sensitivity to the expectations and feelings of others • Heightened self-awareness, accompanied by a feeling of being different • High expectations of self and others, often leading to high levels of frustration with self, others, and situations	• Advanced progression through the developmental milestones • Dyssynchrony or asynchrony may be obvious (e.g., advanced performance in a particular area) • Extraordinary memory • Enjoyment and speed of learning • Early and extensive language development • Fascination with books • Strong need for consistency between abstract values and personal actions • Advanced cognitive and affective capacity for conceptualizing and solving societal problems • Advanced levels of moral judgment	• Curiosity • Excellent sense of humor • Abstract reasoning and problem-solving skills • Vivid imagination (e.g., imaginary companions) • Sensitivity and compassion • Affective precocity may lead to leadership roles and preference for older playmates • Idealism and sense of justice • Earlier development of inner locus of control • Unusual emotional depth and intensity • Ability to develop solutions to social and environmental problems

Adapted from Silverman (1993) and Clark (2013).

skilled at puzzles, Legos, and design activities. Children with high social intelligence are able to create relationships with others (often older peers) and demonstrate empathy that their peers generally will not perceive (Piirto, 2007, p. 225). These talent areas should be recognized and planned for educationally to further develop special talents.

Considering affective characteristics and social emotional development of children is important when designing programming and interacting with young gifted learners. The various developmental levels within a child may be inconsistent, for example a three-year-old could be cognitively functioning as an eight-year-old while emotionally functioning at the three-year-old level. Additional factors such as trauma, emotional or physical instability, and poverty have shown to impact a child's development and should also be recognized and addressed.

If we focus on the developmental and affective characteristics of giftedness, educators and parents will develop the ability to understand the unique needs of these learners. Silverman (1993) explained that "giftedness has an emotional as well as a cognitive substructure: cognitive complexity gives rise to emotional depth. Thus, gifted children not only *think* differently from their peers, they also *feel* differently" (p. 3). The use of case studies in the upcoming chapters illustrates how these characteristics and developmental traits manifest in some children at young ages, while providing focus on specific strategies for use in the classroom.

There are many extraordinary stories about children exhibiting advanced abilities and how the adults in their lives worked with them to further develop their talent. For example, the well-known inventor Thomas Edison experienced challenges during his education due to his voracious curiosity and asking "why?" of his teachers, but also due to the fact that he was deaf in one ear and 80 percent deaf in the other. To address his curiosity, he devoured both scientific works and classical texts at the local library. His advanced reading activity was further motivated by his father who paid him a dime per piece. His mother, Nancy, an educator herself, guided much of Edison's early instruction and worked with him to compensate for his disability, and his parents also engaged a science tutor as he learned physics (Beals, 1997).

Albert Einstein had early exposure to science as his father ran a battery factory in Germany. He enjoyed exploring the workings of the compass from the age of five, but he was not the most vocal of children. Einstein reflectively believed that the Prussian education system stifled creativity and focused on rote skills, and since his family had a medical student boarding with them, he had the opportunity to have many meaningful conversations with their resident student boarder about popular books on physical science (Encyclopedia Britannica, Britannica.com). Einstein started playing the violin at age six, and continued to play throughout his life, and by the age of 12, Einstein had already composed several songs. He also engaged in many humanitarian actions later in life including funding and developing a university in Israel. The interplay of physical, cognitive, and affective development is important in developing gifts and talents. Using case studies to consider the interplay can build understanding and knowledge in applying what is known to support children in their social and emotional growth to further talent development.

Cultural Considerations and Giftedness Across Cultures

"Gifted students come from all racial, ethnic, and cultural populations as well as all economic strata" (NAGC, 2019). The impact of various cultural backgrounds upon school achievement has been found to begin early among diverse individuals with gifts and talents (Ford, 2010). Due to bias, culturally, linguistically, and economically diverse gifted children are not easy to identify (Rimm, Siegle, & Davis, 2018). Students who are Black and Latino, receive free/reduced-price lunch, and/or are English language learners, were less likely to be identified as gifted, even when their achievement was on a par with their peers (Siegle et al., 2015). Low-income socio-economic status among high-ability learners has an effect upon exposure to early learning opportunities. Disparities between children from lower-income families and their higher-income peers are evident starting in first grade due to lack of access to preschool programs and other resources that support cognitive development and educational readiness.

Learning Opportunities

Almost 90 years of longitudinal studies about the gifted revealed that children who make considerable advances from a young age do better than equally bright individuals who have not made early advances and better than individuals of lesser aptitude (Colangelo, Assouline, & Gross, 2004). When learning opportunities for gifted children are correctly matched with their current developmental levels, the child will excel in talent development throughout their childhood and adulthood. With appropriate educational experiences, good parenting, healthy friendships, and active spirituality, early childhood can be the beginning of lifelong flourishing for gifted individuals (Sayler, 2009).

It is important to recognize the need to participate in challenging early learning experiences that are designed to match the learner's characteristics. Studies suggest that young learners are able to reach higher levels of understanding using teaching strategies and pedagogical approaches from gifted education with challenging learning experiences. These instructional approaches are critical for the gifted and when they benefit all students then there is no reason why they should not be implemented.

Policy makers, educators, and parents should actively seek research-based practices to use with advanced and gifted children to maximize opportunities for growth. Gifted children benefit from open, complex tasks when their learning process is externally guided. Learners who are provided with opportunities to experiment learned more, experienced more "flow" (full immersion in an activity), and felt more positive toward the task than those who were not given this opportunity, but only when they were guided through the inquiry cycle by prompts to generate hypotheses, perform experiments, and draw conclusions (Eysink, Gersen, & Gijlers, 2015). Identification in detecting advanced ability at early ages can be challenging and controversial as there are concerns related to child development and the lack of appropriate testing protocols.

Transitioning into a formal educational program is a major change in children's educational lives. When young gifted children transition from preschool to school, the details that really matter include understanding the background to the transition; the experiences of the learning environment in the home, in the preschool, and in the school; and the experiences of relationships with the educator and age-peers, and facilitating continuity of communication between environments (Grant, 2013). In observing child-educator relationships, the most supportive of these relationships combined emotional security and high levels of intellectual stimulation.

When at home, parents of gifted children reported that learning experiences were intense and enthusiastic with child and parent opportunities that focused on guidance about learning goals and activities/experiences to develop specific understanding or skills. This sounds very formal when in fact these experiences and activities often include hands-on activities building on specific areas of interest for the child. This kind of learning support has been identified as typical in the home lives of gifted children, but not so with children the same age. When looking more generally at preschool learning experiences, there was little similarity with the home learning experiences and often a significant difference between the environments.

Programming

While the home environment is the starting place for a young child's early learning, early childhood education involves formalized and intentional planning for developing a child's purposeful growth (Hertzog & Gadzikowski, 2017). Curriculum planning is crucial when examining the association between early childhood education and gifted education (Barbour & Shakelee, 1998). Understanding appropriate approaches to learning in the field of gifted education includes exposure to advanced thinking processes, opportunities for creativity, conceptual development, and inquiry.

All children need to learn specific social emotional learning skills. With advanced and high-functioning young children it is important that adults spend the time to teach specific SEL (social and emotional learning) skills because often there is a level of sensitivity and awareness at a younger age. These skills provide strategies for these learners as they work to understand advanced concepts, make connections to the real world, interact with other students, and address individual sensitivities.

Learning begins the moment each child is born and an advanced child begins to gain valuable skills that will develop and grow throughout their lifetime. Quality learning experiences build the foundation for healthy adjustment and learning. Whether those experiences are gained at home or in a school-based program, early childhood professionals know the importance of tending to early developmental stages and that quality preparation will reap rewards later. Early childhood is an influential time as much is happening in the brain and central nervous system beginning at birth and throughout the coming years. A child's early experiences can have a significant impact on their development and learning. It is important for parents, caretakers, and educators in early learning centers and schools to work cooperatively during the crucial first years and collaborate across the child's day. All children regardless of socio-economic status need to have access to quality programming and experiences.

This book defines, describes, and discusses the social and emotional development of young gifted children. The first section of the book provides an introduction and definitions across the various developmental phases of children. The second section focuses on characteristics of the social and emotional development of children and the third section explains the developmental characteristics described in the second section by providing a series of case studies about advanced children in the various stages of early childhood with descriptive observational examples. The final section focuses on describing and providing insight in addressing and working with children as they develop skills for evolving inter- and intra-relationships, building friendships, and regulating themselves, and includes a list of resources.

Discussion Questions

1. Consider your childhood experiences and reflect upon your interactions with influential adults. Who influenced your sense of self and to what effect? What were some positive and negative messages that you remember receiving?
2. As an adult, when talking with other adults, what differences do you notice when they speak about helping young children develop positive and healthy interactions with themselves? What types of purposeful learning experiences are important? What good ideas have you heard?
3. In your influential role with young people, what personal view of themselves would you like to influence through your interactions with them? What social emotional learning lessons for young children are important to you?

Bibliography

Adelson, J. L., McCoach, D. B., & Gavin, M. K. (2012). Examining the effects of gifted programming in mathematics and reading using the ECLS-K. *Gifted Child Quarterly*, *56*(1), 25–39. https://doi.org/10.1177/0016986211431487.

Arslan, S., & Demirtas, Z. (2016). Social emotional learning and critical thinking disposition. *Studia Psychologica*, *58*(4), 276–285. https://doi.org/10.21909/sp.2016.04.723.

Barbour, N. E., & Shaklee, B. D. (1998). Gifted education meets Reggio Emilia: Visions for curriculum in gifted education for young children. *Gifted Child Quarterly*, *42*(4), 228.

Beals, G. (1997). www.thomasedison.com.

Casa, T. M., Gavin, M. K., Firmender, J. M., & Carroll, S. R. (2017). Kindergarteners' achievement on geometry and measurement units that incorporate a gifted education approach. *Gifted Child Quarterly*, *61*(1), 52–72. https://doi.org/10.1177/0016986216671806.

Chunyan, Y., Bear, G. G., & May, H. (2018). Multilevel associations between school-wide social-emotional learning approach and student engagement across elementary, middle, and high schools. *School Psychology Review*, *47*(1), 45–61. https://doi.org/10.17105/SPR-2017-0003.V47-1.

Clark, B. (1992). *Growing up gifted* (4th ed.). Macmillan Publishing.

Clark, B. (2013). *Growing up gifted: Developing the potential of children at home and at school* (8th ed.). Pearson Education South A.

Cohen, J., Onunaku, N., Clothier, S., & Poppe, J. (2005). *Helping young children succeed: strategies to promote early childhood social and emotional development*. National Conference of State Legislatures and Zero to Three. www.cde.ca.gov/sp/cd/re/itf09socemodev.asp.

Colangelo, N., Assouline, S., & Gross, M. (2004). *A nation deceived: How schools hold back America's brightest students*. Connie Belin & Jacqueline N. Blank International Center for Gifted Education and Talent Development.

Colangelo, N., & Fleuridas, C. (1986). The abdication of childhood. *Journal of Counseling & Development*, *64*(9), 561.

Durlak, J. A. (2016). Programme implementation in social and emotional learning: Basic issues and research findings. *Cambridge Journal of Education*, *46*(3), 333–345. https://doi.org/10.1080/0305764X.2016.1142504.

Encyclopedia Britannica. www.Britannica.com.

Eysink, T. H., Gersen, L., & Gijlers, H. (2015). Inquiry learning for gifted children. *High Ability Studies*, *26*(1), 63–74. https://doi.org/10.1080/13598139.2015.1038379.

Ford, D. (2010). Underrepresentation of culturally different students in gifted education: reflections about current problems and recommendations for the future. *Gifted Child Today*, *33*(3), 31–35.

Grant, A. (2013). Young gifted children transitioning into preschool and school: What matters? *Australasian Journal of Early Childhood*, *38*(2), 23–31.

Greenberg, M. T., Domitrovich, C. E., Weissberg, R. R., & Durlak, J. A. (2017). Social and emotional learning as a public health approach to education. *Future of Children*, *27*(1), 13–32.

Gregory, A., & Fergus, E. (2017). Social and emotional learning and equity in school discipline. *Future of Children, 27*(1), 117–136.

Harrison, C. (2003). Giftedness in early childhood: The search for complexity and connection. *Roeper Review, 26*(2), 78–84.

Hertzog, N., & Gadzikowski, A. (2017). *Early childhood gifted education: Fostering talent development.* National Association for Gifted Children.

Housman, D. (2017). The importance of emotional competence and self-regulation from birth: A case for the evidence-based emotional cognitive social early learning approach. *International Journal of Child Care & Education Policy, 11*(1), 1–19. https://doi.org/10.1186/s40723-017-0038-6.

Lim, T. (2009). Early identification. In B. Kerr (ed.), *Encyclopedia of giftedness, creativity, and talent* (pp. 273–275). SAGE Publications.

Maras, M. A., Thompson, A. M., Lewis, C., Thornburg, K., & Hawks, J. (2015). Developing a tiered response model for social-emotional learning through interdisciplinary collaboration. *Journal of Educational & Psychological Consultation, 25*(2/3), 198–223. https://doi.org/10.1080/10474412.2014.929954.

McDevitt, T. M., & Ormrod, J. E. (2013). *Child development and education* (5th ed.). Pearson.

Meyers, A. B., Tobin, R. M., Huber, B. J., Conway, D. E., & Shelvin, K. H. (2015). Interdisciplinary collaboration supporting social-emotional learning in rural school systems. *Journal of Educational & Psychological Consultation, 25*(2/3), 109–128. https://doi.org/10.1080/10474412.2014.929956.

NAEYC. (2009). NAEYC position statement: Developmentally appropriate practice in early childhood programs serving children from birth through age 8. www.naeyc.org/sites/default/files/globally-shared/downloads/PDFs/resources/position-statements/dap-statement_0.pdf.

NAGC. (2019). NAGC position statement: A definition of giftedness that guides best practice. https://www.nagc.org/sites/default/files/Position%20Statement/Definition%20of%20Giftedness%20%282019%29.pdf

Neihart, M., Pfeiffer, S., & Cross, T. (2016). *The social and emotional development of gifted children: What do we know?* (2nd ed.). Prufrock Press.

Oberle, E., Domitrovich, C. E., Meyers, D. C., & Weissberg, R. P. (2016). Establishing systemic social and emotional learning approaches in schools: A framework for schoolwide implementation. *Cambridge Journal of Education*, *46*(3), 277–297. https://doi.org/10.1080/03 05764X.2015.1125450

Pfeiffer, S. I., & Petscher, Y. (2008). Identifying young gifted children using the gifted rating scales—Preschool! Kindergarten form. *Gifted Child Quarterly*, *52*(1), 19–29.

Piirto, J. (2007). The young talented child from birth to grade two. In *Talented children and adults: Their development and education*, third edition (pp. 220–259). Prufrock Press.

Play, toys, learning, and understanding an interview with Doris Borgin. (2016). *American Journal of Play*, *8*(2), 145–156. www.museumofplay .org/app/uploads/2022/01/8-2-interview-play-toys-learning-and-understanding.pdf

Rimm, S., Siegle, D., & Davis, G. (2018). *Education of the gifted and talented* (7th ed.). Pearson.

Sayler,M.F. (2009). Gifted and thriving: A deeper understanding of meaning of GT. In L. V. Shavininia (ed.), *International handbook on giftedness*. Springer.

Schonert-Reicht, K. A. (2017). Social and emotional learning and teachers. *Future of Children*, *27*(1), 137–155.

Siegle, D., Gubbins, E. J., O'Rourke, P., Dulong Langley, Mun, R. U., Luria, S. R., Little, C. A., McCoach, D. B., Knupp, T., Callahan, C. C., & Plucker, J. A. (2016). Barriers to underserved students' participation in gifted programs and possible solutions. *Journal for the Education of the Gifted*, *39*, 103–131.

Silverman, L. (1993). *Counseling the gifted and talented*. Love.

White, A., Moore, D. W., Fleer, M., & Anderson, A. (2017). A thematic and content analysis of instructional and rehearsal procedures of preschool social emotional learning programs. *Australasian Journal of Early Childhood*, *42*(3), 82–91. https://doi.org/10.23965/AJEC.42.3.10.

Wilson, H. E. (2015). Patterns of play behaviors and learning center choices between high ability and typical children. *Journal of Advanced Academics*, *26*(2), 143–164. https://doi.org/10.1177/1932 202X15577954.

2

Overview of Social Emotional Learning in Early Childhood

Incredibly, a newborn's brain and overall size doubles in the first year of life and keeps growing to about 80 percent of adult size by age three and 90 percent, nearly full grown, by age five. This early brain development during the early years has been characterized in pediatric neuroscience as "blossoming" in which some of the most dynamic and elaborate growth changes occur within the brain, as discovered from medical research with brain imaging and specific biological processes. Different areas of the brain are responsible for different abilities like movement, language, and emotion and develop at different rates. As children age, different areas of the brain have been found to have greater activity during the preschool and kindergarten years. Dependent upon a specific task, a larger number of brain regions seem to be required at younger ages than at older ages for successful completion of the same cognitive task, suggesting that as anatomical and physiological changes occur, the existence of "scaffolding" mechanisms in the early cerebral functions are eliminated with increased age (Brown & Jernigan, 2012). The preschool years are a dynamic developmental period dominated by growth, construction, and "blossoming" that will later be pruned and tuned with maturation and experience. Noninvasive structural and functional neuroimaging methods have revolutionized how the brain is studied but the preschool and early childhood years remain

DOI: 10.4324/9781003353690-2

relatively under-characterized as compared to other periods of development across all types of neuroimaging. This is most commonly believed to be due to image scans being easier to complete with infants while sleeping and with older children, seven years and above, who are in the young school-age range and more accustomed to following directions. The greater difficulty of collecting neuroimaging data with preschool-age children also provides information related to the nature of brain-behavior relationships during these years and the need for expressing the developing brain with outward behaviors.

Every experience excites neural circuits and the production of brain cells. Brain connections interact in more complex ways and build more complex capabilities within a child. The early years of a child's life are a crucial time for making connections. By providing a rich environment with good nutrition, sleep routines, play, social and emotional support, and love throughout infancy and early childhood, a child can make more connections.

What happens to children in the first five years of life provides the foundation for a lifetime. By the time students enter elementary school, too many school-age children carry invisible backpacks weighted with past stressors of fears, worries, unmet needs, anxiety, trauma, sadness, anger, loneliness, and more. This book focuses on supporting the healthy development of young children in the hope of mitigating those concerns among children with advanced intellectual abilities and providing parents, educators, and caretakers with information to help a bright child thrive from the early years onward.

As a new mother (Bronwyn) welcoming our first child three weeks into the global pandemic, there were mixed feelings about the lack of interactions with people at that time. At the start of life, our baby was only meeting medical personnel wearing masks for newborn wellness visits and not meeting family or friends due to pandemic recommendations to isolate and stay at home. With wide eyes, our baby would look at us closely when we donned our masks to leave home. Finally, with much precaution, we visited my mother and introduced our baby to her. They immediately took to each other and began a happy smiling, giggling relationship. I knew that if we could get them together, they would effervesce at one another! While I was concerned about interacting with others due to the contagiousness of the pandemic, I was also concerned about not interacting with others as related to the social and emotional development of our young baby. Two years after the pandemic, the impact of isolation on individuals has been studied and it is well understood that humans are social beings who thrive on social interaction. Long before the pandemic, it was also well known that babies need their mothers to provide nurturing affection and love to thrive and grow.

Many people love to watch babies, whether singletons or twins, and it is frequently noted with twins that they continue to cuddle close and keep a hand or foot on one another to stay connected. But, singleton babies also exhibit this phenomenon with their caretaker. As a new mother, I frequently observed and commented to my husband that our baby was staying connected through touch by keeping a hand or foot on one of us to be close. Babies need ample physical touch and emotional engagement to survive and thrive. Children who have not had gentle attention are at a higher risk for behavioral, emotional, and social problems as they grow up (Harmon, 2010). Adult responsiveness teaches infants about trust and babies learn through their interactions with adults that their actions affect others' responses. Infants with mothers who are quick to imitate their babies behaviors develop more rapidly. The development of young children is a complex series of interactions, experiences, nutrition, sleep, and more. Indeed there are many books and articles focused on specific areas of child development such as nutrition, sleep, play, behavior, language, potty training, and more. Focusing on a specific topic can be helpful for parents when uncertain about how to proceed in a given area. But it is also important to recognize that just as the pandemic demonstrated the need for social interaction while also staying safe, so too, it is important to recognize that a child's social and emotional understanding develops in the context of their whole life as a complete person.

What is social and emotional learning among children? As part of human development, children acquire and apply knowledge and skills to understand themselves, manage emotions, and achieve their goals. This includes developing relationships with others, feeling and showing empathy toward others, and making responsible decisions. These understandings and attitudes contribute to success in activities not only in educational experiences but throughout life.

Research about social and emotional learning (SEL) has grown extensively over the past two decades (Niemi, 2020). While individual competence and skill among children and young people remains the primary emphasis, the focus within SEL has expanded to include interactions among individuals to create caring environments in schools and communities. When children have their physical and emotional needs met, they can focus better on their academic development as well. To understand the connections between families and friends, both in their neighborhood and at school, children must have opportunities to observe relationships, attitudes, and behaviors, and are then better prepared to succeed in school-based activities. Social and emotional learning encompasses the thinking skills, behavioral skills, and regulatory skills needed to interact successfully with others (McKown, 2017).

Professional educational associations have shone their platform spotlights on the importance of recognizing the development of the whole child. The Association of Supervision and Curriculum Development (ASCD) focused on the development of the whole child with the ASCD Whole Child Initiative and approach to education that would promote long-term development and success and support for schools and communities with five tenets that move schools beyond defining educational success as only academic achievement. These five tenets, healthy, safe, engaged, supported, and challenged, provide the focus of ASCD partnerships with schools for improving the learning environment and the *ASCD Whole Child Action Plan Guide* is available online (https://library.ascd.org/m/1f2720c1c2296a94/original/ASCD-Whole-Child-Action-Plan-Guide.pdf). The National Association of Gifted Children (NAGC) formed the NAGC Whole Gifted Child Task Force, which produced the *NAGC WGC Task Force Report* (https://files.eric.ed.gov/fulltext/ED600216.pdf)

with the charge "to present knowledge and research about the diversity of gifted children, their needs, development, and the importance of providing alternatives for their ongoing growth in school, home, and community" (NAGC WGC Task Force Report, 2018).

The WGC Task Force Report (2018) identified understandings about the multidimensional nature of gifted individuals, what is known about what might affect gifted individuals' experiences, and provided practical and proactive recommendations to foster the development of emotional health, engagement, achievement, relationships, and meaning in life. When considering the nature of giftedness as an individual human experience, the professional literature indicates particular areas of concern for gifted populations:

> Gifted learners may be at a greater risk of developing behavioral or emotional problems due to such factors as asynchronous development, extremely high or unrealistic expectations of parents and teachers, lack of access to cognitive peers, heightened sensitivities and intensities, nonconformity, and a mismatch between their abilities and educational environment. These issues may pose additional demands and stress not only on the gifted learner, but on the parents or caregivers as well.

By exploring giftedness with perspectives from parents, consultants, educators, counselors, academics, and advocates, the WGC Task Force provided broad recommendations to inform identification practices, programs, and services for gifted students:

> (1) Recognize that giftedness in children exists as part of the human experience and can be demonstrated in a variety of contexts; (2) Recognize the compatibility of developing healthy coping strategies, well-being, and a strong sense of self alongside talent areas; (3) Recognize that gifted children have the right to an identity beyond their talent area; (4) Provide universal screening with valid

and reliable measures of verbal and nonverbal reasoning; (5) In addition to universal screeners, utilize identification procedures that provide a holistic profile; (6) Provide programs and services that match specific areas of gifts and needs in a manner that are thoughtfully planned in advance and address a variety of factors, including noncognitive and co-cognitive factors that affect the development of a gifted child; (7) Provide programs and services that are unique relative to those provided by curricular approaches in regular classroom settings; (8) Develop opportunities, time, and resources for personalized learning to support the deep exploration of individual interests, passions, and ideas; and (9) Ensure the focus of programs and services is on developing strengths rather than solely addressing deficits.

(pp. 3–4)

To understand the advanced development of young children who are not yet identified as gifted and talented, parents and professionals can benefit from an understanding of typical developmental milestones for the age of a child as well as recognizing what is typical for their child. In most public educational systems, children are not identified for gifted and talented programs until second grade and beyond. When children are finally identified as gifted and talented at older ages, the assessment protocols used provide professionals with information about how far advanced a child may be for their age. For example, intelligence tests and other cognitive assessments may indicate that a particular child may be one to three years beyond their age level, in which case, appropriate gifted services may be recommended and delivered for the child to benefit and have their academic needs met. Likewise, in sports, it is common for coaches to determine a young athlete's level of performance and provide additional talent development opportunities with sports camps, individual practice sessions, and other coaching opportunities. But during the very young early childhood years, recognizing and identifying advanced talents are largely left to parents.

Learning Experiences for Advanced Young Children

For parents and professionals who have the opportunity to provide advanced experiences to young children who demonstrate early readiness and interest, much can be learned from across the professional fields of education, psychology, and medicine. In gifted education curriculum and instruction literature, the role of acceleration for advanced learners provides an intervention to match a child's higher performance level of functioning to the level of their learning experiences for a better match (VanTassel-Baska, 2022). When elementary children are identified for gifted programmatic services by their potential and performance indicators, typical instruments may show that a learner may be one to two years advanced above their grade level and that it would be appropriate for them to work with materials that are one to two years above their classmates' curricular learning experiences. Offering learning experiences where very young children enjoy their creativity with imaginative play, laughter, cross-disciplinary connections, and making real-world connections can adapt best practices from gifted education literature with thoughtful applications for young children. By definition, individuals with gifts and talents are capable of outstanding achievements (Marland Report, 1972). With appropriate supports, teachers, and learning experiences, gifted children can learn far beyond the level of their age-mates (Cross, Cross, & Andersen, 2017), and within the context of overall support for the growth and development of gifted children, affective learning experiences should address intrapersonal and interpersonal knowledge, beliefs, attitudes, and behaviors that contribute to personal self-understanding and acceptance, as well as foster positive interactions with others, and enhance personal abilities to approach and respond to talent development opportunities and challenges. When addressing social and emotional development, applying a psychological theory to create a foundation for learning activities undergirds and provides groundwork for planning activities. When students with exceptional potential lack the psychosocial skills needed to overcome impediments to their achievement, such as resilience in the face of failure, resistance to peer pressure, and the like, it is a loss to society (Subotnik et al., 2011).

One day, I (Bronwyn) was standing in a checkout line behind a well-mannered, quiet young boy who looked up at me while waiting for his adult to return to the checkout line, I smiled at him and said "Hello" as he smiled back. The adult returned to the line and began berating the child who looked bewildered as to why he was being talked to so harshly. The adult continued to fuss at the child as they left the store and the cashier remarked, "He wasn't doing anything." The moment stayed in my mind and upon return to the store a few days later, I brought it up to a different cashier and supervisor at the checkout line. The supervisor didn't say anything while the cashier shook her head and said, "We see that sort of thing all the time, some people." It is moments like these that can clarify what adults can do to help children develop their personal social and emotional understanding. If adults can provide positive attention, quality interactions, and appropriate learning experiences when working with young children, healthy psychosocial skills can be built and developed to help young people navigate difficult moments when they interact with others and decide how to handle their situations. The tone and way that adults speak to children is the internal voice that stays with a child as they grow (Dolcos & Albarracín, 2014). Children grow into adults who are influenced by the behaviors of adults they know well. To change or break the cycle of a stressful climate and organizational culture, it is a continual process for professionals and caregivers to encourage respect, dignity, and love for self and for one another. By helping children learn to take care of their minds and bodies, we can be caregivers who model taking care of ourselves to better care for others.

Organizational Culture and Climate: At Home and in Educational Settings

During the global pandemic when many people worked from home, there was a humorous cartoon that if a person didn't care for their work environment in their own home, it was on them to fix their climate and culture. At the professional level, it is well understood that organizational culture and climate has an impact on employee work productivity, satisfaction, and the employer's attrition and turnover rate. Indeed, the enjoyment of being in a healthy home and work climate and culture may not be noticed until someone has a negative experience of being within an unhealthy organizational climate and culture. The environment where a child spends many of their hours, whether at home or in a care or educational facility, can have a huge impact on their social and emotional development and health. School climate and culture has a significant impact upon the educators and students within the school setting and the climate and culture of a home has significant impact on the overall well-being of those in the home. To create a healthy climate at home or in an educational setting to support growth and learning, adults should understand the characteristics of child development in early childhood and the right learning experiences, techniques, and toys or manipulatives to provide to a developing child.

Psychosocial Development

Whether at home, in care facilities, or in school settings, young children need a secure environment where they feel safe, loved, cared for with appropriate attention, and nurtured. According to the psychologist Erik Erikson's stage theory of psychosocial development, individuals enter stages where they experience a series of crises over time with their interactions with others (Erikson, 1968, 1950/1995). Understanding Erikson's stages can help caretakers increase their awareness about the social and emotional learning that a young child is experiencing. In the first stage of development, infants face the crisis of *basic trust versus basic mistrust*. Caregivers who respond to their infants' needs teach babies to trust the world, while infants also come to know that their needs may not always be met immediately. As a new mother in the hospital, I remember a nurse saying, "Babies are not manipulators. You can't love and hold them too much." Some parents may think that a baby is crying to manipulate them but that is not the case and it is important to not confuse baby and toddler behaviors. When a cry is heard, a baby is communicating the only way they have that a need should be tended to. All babies need tending to and love in order to build their sense of trust in others. The essential strength or virtue that results from this crisis is an outcome of *hope*.

An example at home or in a daycare setting of how caretakers may influence a child's trust level is their level of responsiveness to a baby's cries for specific needs such as hunger, discomfort, loneliness, etc. When a baby's needs are quickly met, feelings of trust and hope that they will be tended to the next time they experience discomfort begin to build.

As toddlers, children become aware of their power to act on their own. In the second stage of development, the crisis of *autonomy versus shame and doubt*, toddlers learn that they can take actions they desire to take, but they may be thwarted in their desire for autonomy by others, such as parents or siblings, who keep them from doing what they want to do. The virtue result is *will-power*. But as they learn what they are capable of doing, interference by others "foreign over control" may reduce confidence and self-assurance, and create doubt in their ability to act on their own.

An example of what this stage and crisis might look like at home could be choosing a specific drawer for the child to hold the little one's bowls and cups with lids, fruit packs, baby food, and baby snacks like "crunchies." As a baby grows into a toddler and sees where their bowls and cups and snacks are regularly kept, they learn a routine and strive to build independence by going to get their own cup and bowl when they are hungry or thirsty.

In this stage, children need attention and if they do not receive positive attention, they will seek attention in ways that adults view negatively. To a child, some form of attention is better than no attention. Imagine two buckets that children need filled on a daily basis, one is called Attention and the other Power. By providing opportunities for children to gain power through activities like picking their spoons and clothes, they have opportunities to "fill" their power bucket needs by making personal choices. Caregivers should regularly "fill" young children's attention bucket needs with positive conversations and feedback.

ATTENTION

POWER

Preschool age children are capable of creating plans and acting on them and face the third crisis of *initiative versus guilt*. While toddlers may simply want to break free of others to act on their own, preschoolers are capable of involving others in their plans, imagining possibilities, and making them happen. When this initiative is struck down by adults or the inability to make their idea happen, a child may feel frustration and even guilt if unable to achieve their goal. Erikson (1950/1995) pointed out that this is a critical stage for the building of society, because

> the child is at no time more ready to learn quickly and avidly, to become bigger in the sense of sharing obligation and performance, than during this period of his development. He is eager and able to make things cooperatively, to combine with other children for the purpose of constructing and planning, and he is willing to profit from teachers and to emulate ideal prototypes.
>
> (p. 232)

Preschools that support children's growing initiative help to create a dynamic society in which individuals work together to achieve great things. The basic virtue that is a lasting outcome of this third crisis is *purpose*. To consider what this crisis might look like on a regular day at home, a child might enjoy listening to music ensemble groups but is unable to produce the same musical result at home and becomes frustrated with their instrument but with regular exposure to playing music may develop a desire for a family band with many sounds playing together.

Children develop a sense of competence as they learn how to work and use tools to be productive during the fourth crisis of *industry versus inferiority* which typically occurs as children enter school. When school-aged children are not successful at developing skills that they are attempting to learn, then they can develop feelings of inferiority. As they learn to cooperate, they also compare their abilities to others and begin to develop the basic virtue of *competence*. Continuing with the example from the previous stage about music development, a child might learn that another child has more or less musical skills than they do and begin to consider their own performance level and talent growth. The same awareness of competency and comparison could apply with other skills that a child enjoys in sports, the arts, and academically.

All of these details of self-knowledge about who they can trust, what they can do independently, when to take initiative, and how well they can do what they are asked to do coalesce during adolescence to form a sense of identity, and the fifth crisis of *identity versus role confusion*. This stage firms an individual's beliefs about themselves and their values which can result in a sense of consistency about who they are and the basic virtue of *fidelity* to their beliefs about themselves and their values. As a child becomes an adolescent, this awareness might become evident as they decide which activities they want to spend their time pursuing and what groups they associate with and value more over time.

As individuals develop a firm sense of self and who they are, they begin to prepare for significant relationships ranging from becoming involved with a romantic partner to becoming committed to an organized purpose such as a theological group, favorite activity, or movement. Young adults in the sixth crisis stage face feelings of *intimacy versus isolation*, in which they determine their level of commitment to another and the separation that would come from not fully participating in the relationship. The essential strength to come from this crisis is *love*. This awareness becomes more evident as adolescents continue friendships, as well as develop romantic interests and relationships (Erikson, 1968, 1950/1995).

Erikson also observed in his patients what he referred to as "residue" from earlier crises in which an individual may have passed through a crisis with an unbalanced experience of too much or not enough of both sides of a crisis which could then result in imbalance in a later stage. For example, if a toddler was never provided with moments of autonomy, then as an adult they may become determined to see if they could get away with things. He referred to this imbalance as an "unfavorable ratio" and attempted to address it through psychoanalysis (Erikson, 1968, 1950/1995). In modern times, parents, caretakers, and educators have opportunities to build positive development and develop social and emotional learning experiences by planning an affective curriculum for young children that develops positive psychosocial skills and abilities.

Managing the home environment so that young children can feel safe and secure provides the critical underpinning of their social and emotional development. Babies begin learning on their first day about how they can trust their caretakers and their subsequent development hinges on their learning experiences during their first five years (Brown & Jernigan, 2012). All human bodies have five basic needs to physically survive and thrive: air, water, food, shelter, and sleep. To graphically demonstrate the physiological needs for healthy humans, Abraham Maslow created a pyramid to illustrate a hierarchical growth of mental and behavioral needs.

Maslow's pyramid depicts a hierarchy of needs beginning at the lowest level of human physiological needs to survive and progressing as needs are provided to the next level of safety and security, love and beginning, self-esteem, and ultimately self-actualization at the top of the pyramid.

To translate and extend Maslow's hierarchy of physiological mental and behavioral needs to daily practice with regular actions, adults should consider necessary action steps to assist children with achieving each step on the hierarchy. For example, to provide for physiological needs, caregivers must plan for children to have satisfying meals and snacks in a timely routine schedule with water and bathroom breaks throughout the day. Children must have opportunities to rest in a safe place with

FIGURE 2.1
Maslow's Hierarchy of Needs. Image courtesy of Wikimedia Commons.

clothing that fits weather changes. To provide for safety and security, families and educators should check that the environment is a safe and secure place for the child to thrive and to also check that the child feels that sense of safety and security. To feel love and belonging, adults must welcome children and clearly communicate their appreciation for the child and that the child is a valued member of the family and the learning community. To build self-esteem with a sense of confidence, personal achievement, respect for others, and appreciation for their unique self, adults should provide children with engaging and challenging learning opportunities that ignite their curiosity, imagination, enthusiasm, and provide appropriate feedback to build and encourage. Finally, to contribute to the development of self-actualization with a sense of creativity, spontaneity, acceptance, purpose, and meaning, adults should encourage each student to develop their talents and special abilities. These types of actions taken by adults should be consistent and supportive.

Emotions are a crucially important aspect of our psychological composition and impact how we function. Humans are social beings with emotions that influence our functioning in three areas of life: intrapersonal, interpersonal, and social-cultural

Overview of Social Emotional Learning in Early Childhood ◆ 31

functions. Intrapersonal relates to the role that emotions play within each of us individually. Interpersonal functions refer to the meaning of emotions in our relationship with others in groups. Social and cultural describes the roles and meanings that emotions have to the maintenance and effective functioning of society and cultures at large.

In psychology and education, three categories frequently referred to include cognitive, affective, and conative. The *cognitive* category includes thinking abilities usually assessed by intelligence tests. Cognitive thinking abilities are the primary focus of schooling. The *affective* category includes emotions and emotional development. Affect regulation refers to people's ability to understand and manage their emotions. *Conation* is related to motivation, such as goal setting, persistence, and personal interests. Since motivational processes involve emotions, many theorists include both affective and conative processes under the general heading of "affective." Relatedly, *affective* learning refers to social and emotional development, and the use of or development of a curriculum with social and emotional learning goals to help students grow in affective dimensions by interacting with others as well as increasing self-awareness.

Social and Emotional Understandings at an Early Age

The mission of the Collaborative for Academic, Social, and Emotional Learning (CASEL) focuses on helping to make evidence-based social and emotional learning an integral part of education from preschool through high school. To better understand social and emotional functioning, CASEL identified and described five competencies as self-awareness, self-management, social awareness, relationship skills, and responsible decision making. Known as the "CASEL Wheel" (https://casel.org/fundamentals-of-sel/what-is-the-casel-framework/), the core competencies focus on the skills and environments that contribute to advancing students' learning and development.

In this section, we provide an overview of the five CASEL competencies and the application of these competencies will be discussed with the case studies in the chapters to follow.

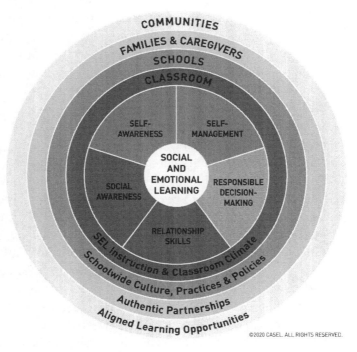

FIGURE 2.2
The CASEL 5 SEL Competencies. Source: ©2021 CASEL. Social and Emotional Learning Framework. All rights reserved. casel.org

Self-awareness is the first competency and includes children correctly identifying their emotions, and how they feel in different situations, having an accurate self-perception, recognizing personal strengths, possessing self-confidence and self-efficacy, which is the personal belief that they can successfully achieve a specific goal.

Have you ever noticed differences in behavior among children in public areas and wondered about differences in parenting? Why do some children run around an open area (that is not a playground setting) shouting while others quietly read near their parents in public settings? What are some children taught about their behavior that others are not? The second CASEL competency is *Self-management*, which includes personal impulse control, stress management, self-discipline, self-motivation, goal setting, and organizational skills. While the second competency focuses on intrapersonal awareness, the third CASEL competency incorporates both interpersonal and social-cultural emotion functions. The third CASEL competency is *Social Awareness* and focuses on the development of perspective-taking, empathy, appreciating diversity, and respect for others.

Relationship Skills is the fourth CASEL competency, which includes personal understanding about communication, social engagement, relationship building, and teamwork. The fifth and final CASEL competency is *Responsible Decision Making* with a focus on identifying problems, analyzing situations, solving problems, evaluating, reflecting, and ethical responsibility.

These five competencies are not learned in a vacuum, but rather the environments where children spend their time have a significant impact on the development of these skills. Children's environments vary from home to school, neighborhoods and community locations, and beyond. The CASEL SEL Framework suggests that schools and school districts contribute to developing these skills and attitudes by establishing equitable learning environments and coordinated opportunities to practice.

Social and Emotional Learning Strategies and Techniques

There are a variety of strategies and instructional techniques that may be used when planning and implementing social and emotional learning experiences with young children. These strategies fit within the categories discussed earlier to match the learning goals related to intrapersonal, interpersonal, and social functioning. To maximize the learning experience, adults should strive to select a strategy that is the closest match to the learning goal. The strategies shown in Table 2.1 will be discussed in the following chapters with concrete examples of how the strategies may fit a particular case study. The selection of a strategy should align to and be appropriate to the child's readiness level. While some strategies may be adapted across the ages discussed within this text of birth to eight years, other strategies are more appropriate for children at the older end of the range who have become school-age children.

34 ◆ Overview of Social Emotional Learning in Early Childhood

TABLE 2.1 Social and Emotional Learning Strategies

SEL Category	SEL Learning Goals	SEL Strategies
Intrapersonal	Self-awareness	Reflections
	Self-management	
	Self-control	Empathy exercises
		Persistence practice
	Self-talk	Emotions
	Individual organization and planning	Goal setting
		Routines
	Role modeling	Role playing
	Impulse control	Mindfulness
		Awareness of attention focus
Intrapersonal	Social awareness and relationship skills	
	Mental flexibility	Creativity
		Play
	Friendship	Helping a child make friends
		Strategies to assist building friendships
		Sharing
	Diversity inclusiveness	
	Relationship skills	
	Role modeling	
	Responsible decision making	
	Problem solving strategies	Critical thinking skills
		Creative thinking skills
	Growth mindset – positive psychology	Definition
		Relevance for children and adults
	Long-range development plan	Talent
		Interest-based

Summary

While it would be risky to make sweeping generalizations about the limited research that has been conducted with advanced young children, there are certain understandings about service practices from the field of gifted education that have been broadly applied when planning learning experiences for children with advanced talents and abilities. These service practices include planning learning opportunities that include acceleration, conceptual development, curricular compacting, higher-level questioning, and advanced opportunities for making connections. In the following chapters, we discuss specific application of these practices with the illustration of case studies throughout early childhood. It is also important to understand that some strategies may apply better with specific ages than with other ages during early childhood.

By teaching young children an introduction to social and emotional understanding, advanced learners can develop initial awareness about their emotions and learn about how they can respond to their emotions in healthy ways. Adults can introduce *intrapersonal behaviors* (self-awareness, self-management, and self-control) and talk about feeling *empathy* for others through stories (such as empathy for the little bear in Goldilocks when she sat on and broke his little chair) and practicing *persistence* when something doesn't work out as expected (such as when a stack of blocks tumbles over). When adults use role modeling to demonstrate practicing self-talk in front of advanced young children, they can see how the adult feels about and handles their own emotions. Adults may role model individual organization and planning by talking about setting a goal (Let's see how high we can stack these blocks and count them!) and consistently using routines such as hand washing before meals and brushing teeth daily. Some strategies such as mindfulness and awareness of focusing our attention help to teach impulse control with school-age children.

Understanding how to apply different strategies with specific ages is critically important for successful learning experiences. For example, developing interpersonal skills includes social awareness and relationship building skills, but using strategies such as developing a long-range talent development plan based on their interests or having a growth mindset from Positive Psychology would be more successful strategies to use with older children who can understand the ideas discussed and how it applies to what they are interested in pursuing. Using playtime productively with creative prompts and toys to build mental flexibility and social awareness can help children learn about sharing toys, playing together, and developing friendships. As friendships develop, using books and stories to talk about sharing, making friends, and taking care of others can help increase children's awareness of building strong relationships with friends. Again, role modeling plays an important role in teaching young children about behaviors. Teaching about how to use responsible decision making and problem solving skills should be talked about through the use of clear and simple language. Including others can be discussed with stories about bullying and inclusiveness and the associated feelings and emotions. Planning learning opportunities to use critical and creative thinking skills should be a hallmark of all activities designed for advanced children. In the chapters to follow, consider the ideas and cases presented and how the strategies may be adapted for local use in homes and educational settings.

Discussion Questions

1. What are some influences upon the psychosocial development of a young child?
2. What environmental details should be present to positively influence the social and emotional development of advanced young children?
3. What are some daily cooperative activities that a child can do to increase their sense of sharing and contributing?

References

Brown, T., & Jernigan, T. (2012). Brain development during the preschool years. *Neuropsychology Review, 22*(4), 313–333. https://www.ncbi.nlm.nih.gov/pmc/articles/PMC3511633/.

Cross, T., Cross, J., & Andersen, L. (2017). The school-based psychosocial curriculum model. In J. VanTassel-Baska & C. Little (Eds.), *Content-based curriculum for high-ability learners* (3rd ed., pp. 383–407). Prufrock Press.

Dolcos, S., & Albarracín, D. (2014). The inner speech of behavioral regulation: Intentions and task performance strengthen when you talk to yourself as a you. *European Journal of Social Psychology, 44,* 636–642.

Erikson, E. (1968). *Identity: Youth and crisis.* W. W. Norton.

Erikson, E. (1995). *Childhood and society.* Vintage Press. (Original work published 1950).

Harmon, K. (2010). How important Is physical contact with your infant? Touch and emotional engagement boost early childhood development, but can children recover from neglectful environments? *Scientific American,* May 6. www.scientificamerican.com/article/infant-touch/

Marland, S. P. 1972. *Education of the gifted and talented. Report to the Congress of the United States by the U.S.* Commissioner of Education. U.S. Government Printing Office.

McKown, C. (2017). *Social and emotional learning: A policy vision for the future. The Future of Children.* Princeton-Brookings. file:///C:/Users/bdmacfarlane/Downloads/foc-policy_brief_spring_2017v5.pdf.

NAGC WGC Task Force. (2018). The whole gifted child task force report to the NAGC to the NAGC board of directors. https://files.eric.ed.gov/fulltext/ED600216.pdf.

Niemi, K. (2020). https://www.the74million.org/article/niemi-casel-is-updating-the-most-widely-recognized-definition-of-social-emotional-learning-heres-why/.

Subotnik, R. F., Olszewski-Kubilius, P., & Worrell, F. C. (2011). Rethinking giftedness and gifted education: A proposed direction forward based on psychological science. *Psychological Science in the Public Interest, 12,* 3–54. doi:10.1177/1529100611418056

VanTassel-Baska, J. (2022). Assumptions about schooling: The myths of advanced learning. *Gifted Child Today, 45*(4), https://doi.org/10.1177/10762175221110939

3

Characteristics and Case Studies of Very Young Children, Birth to Two Years

Parenting gifted and talented children provides unique experiences that differ from other parenting experiences (Papadopoulos, 2021) and parents are typically the first to recognize advanced abilities in their young children. These unique parenting experiences can raise concerns, influence decision making, and increase stress and anxiety about their development (Jolly & Matthews, 2012), and parents can have a significant impact on their child's development, particularly during early childhood, through daily interactions, support, inspiration, and providing a supportive environment (Robinson, 2000), as well as playing a pivotal role in gifted children's social emotional growth (Jolly, Treffinger, Inman, & Smutny, 2011).

In *The Complete and Authoritative Guide Caring for Your Baby and Young Child, Birth to Age 5*, Dr. Shelov clarifies the gifts a child brings to a parent, and the gifts a parent should provide for a child. A child's gifts are powerful enough to change a parent's life positively and include unqualified love, absolute trust, the thrill of discovery, and the heights of emotion. Likewise, a parent has many vital gifts to offer a child and help them become a

DOI: 10.4324/9781003353690-3

healthy, happy, capable individual. The gifts a parent gives to a child include unconditional love, self-esteem, values and traditions, joy in life, good health, secure surroundings, and skills and abilities (Shelov, 2014).

When we consider our best selves as adults, we are usually well-rested and not experiencing feelings of hunger, thirst, discomfort, frustration, anger, sadness, or fear. In regard to behavior and toddler tantrums, with the exception of specific needs, when a child's needs are met, expected behaviors typically follow as well. Behavior is usually a symptom of what need remains to be met. Is the child hungry? Tired? Uncomfortable? When caregivers focus on meeting a need, then the cause of the symptom can be addressed. While children should be allowed to express their emotions and an occasional tantrum is inevitable, parents also want to help children learn to channel strong emotions such as frustration and anger in positive directions away from violent or overly aggressive behavior. As parents observe a child's emotions increasing, it can be helpful to distract and turn their energy and attention to new activities. If distraction is not possible, certain behaviors may be extinguished by ignoring the behavior rather than rewarding it with more attention. In public settings, parents may choose to remove the child to a quieter place to calm down and then return to the activity. Shelov (2014) does not advise the use of physical punishment as it may teach a child that aggression is an acceptable way to respond when they do not get their way. Parents should also refrain from overreacting and complicated explanations. There is a joke that when you see a parent trying to reason with a toddler, you know that the parent is not the one in charge. Set the parameters with clear, simple, straightforward language. If a child hits, bites, kicks, or engages in some other harmful behavior, adults should immediately and clearly tell the child that they are not to do that behavior and move the child off by themselves for a few minutes as a consequence. If too much time goes by before the behavior is addressed, the child will not connect the correction to the behavior.

Developmental Characteristics from Birth to Two Years

Conventional child development indicates that there is exponential growth in the first five years of a child's life. The following two tables have been adapted to showcase typical milestones in the areas of social emotional, cognitive, and language development. The second table provides an overview of toys, activities, and parental behaviors to consider at typical ages. For advanced children, adults can review the next age group in the table and consider the child's milestones and activities as related to their age group. It is possible for caregivers to plan for differentiated learning experiences as needed in early childhood by carefully selecting reading materials, toys, and learning experiences that may be "off-level" or advanced for their age group.

The best way for a two-year-old to learn how to behave around other people is to have plenty of opportunities to be around other people. While parallel play may look anti-social, parents will also notice that favorite games may be imaginative and involve pretending to be like their parents as they put their teddy to bed and use the same words they hear as you model for them how to eat their vegetables, brush their teeth, and take care of themselves. Providing monitored play time with two to three other children helps a child learn how to play with other children, not just the grown-ups in their lives.

The National Association for the Education of Young Children (NAEYC) provides information about the early developmental characteristics during infancy and the toddler years. Growth and development is rapid during this early time and at birth, babies recognize their mothers' and fathers' voices, and during the first 12 months, many changes occur. When a baby turns one year of age, typical social interactions that they enjoy include playing patty-cake (clapping hands) and rolling a ball back and forth, saying mama or dada or a few more words, responding to one-step simple commands, and waving bye-bye (Eisenberg, Murkoff, & Hathaway, 1996, p. 356). At two years of age, parallel play is commonly understood in early childhood development to mean that children play with something beside another person, rather than with a nearby child or adult.

TABLE 3.1 Social Emotional Milestones for Birth to Two Years

Age	Social Emotional Milestones	Cognitive Milestones	Language milestones
One to three months old Note: Babies cannot receive too much love and positive attention.	Begins to develop a social smile. Enjoys playing with other people and may cry when playing stops, becomes more communicative and expressive with their face and body. Imitates some movements and facial expressions.	To stimulate brain growth at this age, provide healthful nutrition. Give consistent, warm, physical contact, be attentive to the baby's rhythms and moods. Provide colorful objects of different shapes, sizes, and tenures to play and explore.	To stimulate brain growth at this age, read children's picture books and family photographs. Speak a foreign language at home.
Four to seven months	Enjoys social play. Interested in mirror images. Responds to other people's expressions of emotion and appears joyful often.	Finds partially hidden objects. Explores with hands and mouth. Struggles to get objects that are out of reach.	Responds to their own name. Begins to respond to "no." Distinguishes emotions by tone of voice. Responds to sound by making sounds. Uses voice to express joy and displeasure. Babbles chains of consonants.
	To stimulate brain growth at this age, watch for cues that your child is ready to meet new people and introduce your child to other children and parents.	To stimulate brain growth at this age, provide a stimulating, safe environment where your baby can begin to explore and roam freely. Give consistent, warm, physical contact and hugs to establish a sense of security and well-being. Be attentive to your baby's rhythms and moods. Respond to your baby when they are upset as well as when they are happy. Engage in rhythmic movement with your child, such as dancing with music. Avoid subjecting your baby to stressful or traumatic experiences, physical or psychological.	To stimulate brain growth at this age, talk and sing to your baby during dressing, bathing, feeding, playing, walking, driving, shopping, etc. Engage in face-to-face talk and mimic your child's sounds to show interest in conversation with your child. Read books to your baby every day together. Point out details in the pictures so that they begin to enjoy and find details and "reading" on their own. If you are able, speak foreign languages at home.

(*Continued*)

TABLE 3.1 (Continued)

Age	Social Emotional Milestones	Cognitive Milestones	Language milestones
Eight to 12 months	Shy or anxious with strangers. Cries when parent leaves. Enjoys imitating people in play. Shows specific preferences for certain people and toys. Tests parental responses to baby's actions during feedings to see parent's response. Tests parental responses to baby's behavior to see parent's response. May be fearful in some situations. Prefers mother or caregiver over all others. Repeats sounds or gestures for attention. Finger feeds self. Extends arm or leg to help when being dressed.	Explores objects in many different ways (shaking, banging, throwing, dropping). Finds hidden objects easily. Looks at correct picture when the image is named. Imitates gestures, Begins to use objects correctly (drinking from cup, brushing hair, dialing phone, listening to receiver).	Pays increasing attention to speech. Responds, to simple verbal requests. Responds to "no." Uses simple gestures, such as shaking head for "no." Babbles with inflection. Says "dada" and "mama." Uses exclamations, such as "oh-oh!" Tries to imitate words.

	Social	Cognitive	Language
One year	Before two years of age, social milestones include: Imitating behavior of others, especially adults and older children. Increasing awareness of self as separate from others. Increasing enthusiasm for company of other children. Demonstrating increasing independence. Beginning to show defiant behavior, particularly with adults with whom they feel comfortable. Increase episodes of separation anxiety, then they fade.	Before two years of age, cognitive milestones include: Finding objects even when hidden under two to three covers. Beginning to sort by shapes and colors. Beginning to play make-believe.	Prior to two years of age, language milestones include: Pointing to an object or picture when it's named for him (where is teddy bear?). Using the names of familiar people. Saying several single words (by 15 to 18 months). Using simple phrases (by eight to 24 months). Following simple instructions. Repeating words overheard in conversation.
Two years	Imitates adults and playmates. Spontaneously shows affections for familiar playmates. Can take turns in games. Understands concepts of "mine" and "his/hers." Expresses affection openly. Expresses a wide range of emotions. Objects to major changes in routine.	Makes mechanical toys work. Matches an object in their hand or room to a picture in a book. Plays make believe with dolls, animals, and people. Sorts objects by shapes and color. Completes puzzles with three or four pieces. Understands the concept of "two."	Follows a two to three part command, such as "Go to your room and bring back your teddy bear and coat." Recognizes and identifies almost all common objects and pictures. Understands most sentences. Understands physical relationships with the words (on, in, and under). Uses four and five word sentences. Can say their name, age, and gender. Uses pronouns (I, you, me, we, they) and some plurals (cars, dogs, trucks). Strangers can understand most of their words.

Adapted from Shelov, 2014.

In the spring of 2022, after two years of the pandemic, babies born at the start of the global pandemic in 2020 were turning two years old and beginning to interact with more people as activities began to open up. With differences in the amounts of exposure to other people and variance in risk tolerance among parents, some children had siblings and larger families to interact with while others were only children with limited interaction with others beyond the home. From the beginning, I (Bronwyn) noticed that our baby exhibited heightened sensitivities. He regularly listened to classical lullabies in his room, was an avid enthusiast for reading books together, and rapidly turned book pages at four months of age. At 12 months, he was interested in the family piano and bouncing to the beat, and at 18 months he became a fan of playing his harmonica and tin cans. He attended a weekly library story time and we enrolled him in a six-week baby exercise movement class. By age two, he expanded his musical instrument repertoire to a tiny accordion, drum and percussion set, bugle, and xylophone. At the two-year birthday, he hit the ceilings of the evaluative scales demonstrating the adaptive and cognitive development of a three-and-a-half-year-old child so we looked into Suzuki level one music records and books to further develop his musical interests. After two years as a new mom isolated during the pandemic, I began to look for and reach out for more interactive opportunities for my young child. I discovered variance in how receptive others were to interacting and frequently was told to wait for my child to be older to participate in an activity with other children. I was disappointed to hear, "We will love to see him in a year when he is older!" "He has to be potty-trained to participate." And what really got me was hearing the response, "I think what he has currently is enough." What do they know? So I reached out to professionals who had provided online Zoom options and received responses that since folks were feeling safer in 2022, they no longer were providing the online live activities and had returned to in-person only opportunities. For advanced children in rural communities who are ready for more experiences, there are limits to opportunities and enforced constraints based on arbitrary age restrictions. Yet, among early childhood research, it is recognized that half of what humans learn is acquired by age five, so what sense does it make to limit the child to waiting to participate in an activity to when they are three or four years instead of beginning at two years of age if they show interest?

Parents and early childhood educators need to balance conventional direction that a child is "too young" for a developmentally appropriate social emotional or cognitive learning activity. It can be all too common for parents to be told by well-meaning educators that their child is too young for an activity when it really depends on the child, the type of activity, the flexibility of the teacher, and the environment of the experience. Since children learn half of what adults understand within the first five years of life, it is not necessary to wait until they are almost that age to begin exposing children to different experiences. Indeed, the likelihood of pursuing various career paths is directly correlated to the amount of exposure to the ideas within the career during childhood.

The National Association for the Education of Young Children (NAEYC) defines developmentally appropriate practice as an approach to teaching that is grounded in research on how young children develop and learn and what is known about the effects of early education (Copple & Bredekamp, 2009). A developmentally appropriate learning experience for a typical young child, or children with exceptional cognitive development, must be meaningful and engaging (Hertzog & Gadzikowski, 2017). Play is the work of childhood. Learning takes place during play and play has many cognitive benefits for both advanced and typical development children. Cognitive benefits include the development of language, creativity, problem-solving, conceptual understanding, and content and process knowledge in the natural sciences. Active, varied, and spontaneous play during the early childhood years lays the foundation for higher-order thinking and formal learning during later years (Hertzog & Gadzikowski, 2017).

Music

Music builds brain connections and helps children develop skills in mathematics, language, emotion regulation, and social awareness. As parents sing and dance and demonstrate enjoyment of music with their baby, they introduce different sounds, beats, and styles of music to children. Infants absorb many sounds in their first few months of life and regular exposure to a variety of musical sounds supports brain development, eye contact, rhythm, smiling, engagement with shaker-type instruments, babbling, and "singing" in response to music. One-year-olds are even more engaged with music than infants, and parents may observe changes in their physical movement as they listen to different tempos of music, move in response to rhythm and the beat, adjust their pitch up and down, distinguish between different instrument voices, play with musical instruments for extended periods of time such as rhythm instruments, drums and other percussion, harmonicas and other wind instruments, and piano keyboards. Two-year-olds may sing along with short phrases of songs and nursery rhymes, enjoy increased time with dancing, marching, jumping, twirling, and other activities while enjoying music simultaneously.

Asynchronous Development

Uneven, or asynchronous, development is a common characteristic among gifted children and it is important for parents and educators to realize that one size does not fit all as advanced children may have variation in their capabilities and skills (NAGC, no date). Asynchrony is the term used to describe the mismatch between cognitive, emotional, and physical development of gifted individuals (Morelock, 1992). Consider the following case studies of two young children in the first and second year of early childhood and the discussions that follow in regard to providing for social and emotional development in concert with their advanced intellectual abilities. Across children's psychology and education, there is not one sure way to raise children with a suggested technique of doing something that will result in a specific outcome. We can take what we know from across the literature and seek to apply the understandings in a thoughtful approach. Consider the following case studies of the baby and the toddler described ahead, an analysis of the situation, and discuss your ideas for the case.

Case Study: Zachary

Zachary is a happy eight-month-old baby boy and the first born child in his family. As an only child, Zachary has mainly interacted with his parents during his first eight months of life, as well as a few neighbors and friends of his parents. Since he lives a distance from his grandparents, he has only met them a few times but regularly meets them online with the computer video meeting tool, Zoom. He has also frequently participated in online video meetings with other groups of people that his parents know both professionally and personally.

Zachary lives in an apartment and both of his parents are working professionals. He regularly listens to music, takes walks in his stroller, and goes for drives in his car seat. He likes being outside and smiles when people speak to him. He listens attentively to his mother and father and likes to be held and rocked by both. He loves to play games like "Peek-A-Boo" and "So Big." He listens to music regularly as there is always music playing softly in the background of his home and he is a good sleeper.

Zachary sleeps in his parents' room in his bassinet and late one night he awoke suddenly when there was a lot of commotion. Beyond their room, they could hear loud noises. Someone was talking and moving in another apartment adjacent to their apartment. For some time, Zachary remained very quiet in his bassinet listening to what was happening. His mother spoke softly to Zachary in a singsong voice and he began to whimper and tear up a bit. His mother cuddled him and began to sing. Zachary's regularly calm nighttime routine had been interrupted by the introduction of loud noises from new neighbors. This new interruption began to occur on a regular basis to not only disrupt Zachary's sleep routine but also to change it so that on the nights when the neighbors were quiet, Zachary still awoke at the time they regularly returned.

Discussion of Zachary's Case

Routines are a basic part of the human body's daily functioning so that when the regular routine is disrupted or a new routine is established, it is important to consider whether the details of the routine are supporting or hindering healthy growth. In Zachary's case, his sleep routine has been disrupted and redesigned anew. Since sleep is a critical factor to a baby's growth and healthy mental functioning, Zachary's parents will want to consider their options to preserve a good night's sleep for their baby Zachary. Perhaps they can get to know the new neighbors and introduce their baby so that their new neighbors can take care to be quiet for the sleeping baby next door. If that is not possible, perhaps rearranging the location of Zachary's bassinet might be something to consider.

Another detail in Zachary's case is his isolation from others. Isolation from grandparents and family who live at a distance can exist in general, not just during pandemic times, and as a result, there is a need to develop local relationships with friends of all ages for the child to interact. There are specific social emotional learning benefits of interacting with people of all ages and learning empathy for different age groups. There are additional socialization benefits for a child receiving focused attention from other adults and listening to them speak. When using internet video calls to speak with family members and others at a distance, parents must also take care in the amount of cell phone usage that their young child is exposed to and observes their parents use. There is heightened concern about the increased use of cell phones and screen time and the impact on young children in terms of socialization, developing empathy concerns for others, and long-term depression. Zachary's parents should plan for authentic interactions with friends to occur in real life more than video interactions that occur on screens for Zachary to socialize more.

As an eight-month-old baby, Zachary's parents should use caution in selecting specific strategies to consider using with him at home and beyond. Since the strategies to be used in home, school, and community settings fall into the categories of intrapersonal (self-awareness, self-management) and interpersonal (social awareness and relationship skills), Zachary's parents can consider role modeling these skills for him to observe. By watching his parents exhibit self-talk about their emotions, their self-awareness, and their self-control, Zachary can begin to make connections to notice when they exhibit empathy for others and persist on task-commitment with their personal activities. Selecting appropriate toys for babies will provide Zachary with variety to stimulate mental flexibility and interact with his parents and caregivers.

His parents might also like to consider keeping a folder full of ideas that they notice are available for children to participate where they live; these kinds of activities may fit into long-range development plans. Inside the home, there are opportunities in many states for parents to connect to local services provided by the public schools and funded by the state. Not only do these parent-home communicator services provide valuable input and thoughtful ideas for parents to consider, they also build an early home to school connection and collaborative relationship between parents and the home to school educator which can provide a foundation for later school success. Many of these programs are available for enrollment at birth. Outside the home, there are different local programs offered in various settings and parents should become connected to the communication resources that provide announcements about various activities coming up for young children to participate. Libraries have reading story time opportunities for young children, many of which begin at birth, and museums have programs related to feelings and emotions conveyed through artwork and the development of artistic interests. Local parks not only provide an important venue for play and creative movement, but there are frequently outdoor music concerts offered for free during warmer months for families to enjoy.

Table 3.2 provides an analysis of some of the behavior needs that Zachary could benefit from and possible strategies for his parents to consider.

50 ◆ Characteristics and Case Studies, Birth to Two Years

TABLE 3.2 Case Analysis for Zachary

Child Name	Behavior Needs Observed	Suggested Strategies
Zachary	• Self-awareness • Relationship skills • Mental flexibility	• Provide appropriate toys for baby challenge • Model and practice physical skills • Daily book reading for at least 30 minutes • Use a baby mirror to model speaking skills and emotional expressions • Model friendships with others • Model routines and problem solving

Case Study: Sylvia

At 22 months, Sylvia is almost two years of age. She is a bright child who enjoys books, music, is highly observant, interested in meeting people but occasionally shy, and energetic. She is well-mannered at home and in public. Her parents do not allow a lot of screen time but they do watch two one-hour music shows each week and they watch videos of friends on social media. In advance of her two-year appointment, she was given a pediatric evaluation and scored with the following results.

Category	Age Score	Off Level Results
Cognitive	30 months	Eight months above age
Adaptive	28 months	Six months above age
Language	18 months	Four months below age
Social Emotional	17 months	Five months below age
Physical	13 months	Nine months below age

Her parents provide many books and experiences for her but have concerns about how to provide more physical and social emotional development opportunities for Sylvia. Like many parents, they have goals for her but they also have concerns about how to achieve those goals.

The first concern for Sylvia's parents is the desire for Sylvia to have friends to play with and develop social skills and friendships with peers. However, since Sylvia recently moved, her parents did not know many parents with children who are Sylvia's age. During the public outings where Sylvia has the opportunity to meet other children, Sylvia's mother observed some of the other children were running, yelling, and hitting others. Sylvia's parents want her to have friends and peers but do not want her to pick up behaviors of hitting, yelling, etc. Some of the parents yell at the children and exhibit behaviors that Sylvia's parents don't want her to experience yet. They took Sylvia to the local splash pad and walked through intense adult relationship conflict near the entrance. Once inside, Sylvia was surprised by the running and yelling of larger children. A few days later, she did not want to return to the splash pad.

The second concern for Sylvia's parents is that her mother learned from a neighborly onlooker that the person who was hired as their babysitter was observed speaking harshly to Sylvia in a public setting. The babysitter had been asked to pick up Sylvia after "school," which is a daycare setting, and watch her for two hours. The neighborly onlooker reported that the babysitter loudly fussed at Sylvia who listened quietly to the babysitter's strong words.

Discussion of Sylvia's Case

Positive emotional relationships at home are mimicked by children, and conversely, negative emotional relationships at home are also mimicked. As Mark Twain wrote, "Children are natural mimics who act like their parents despite every effort to teach them good manners." There are some realities of life that children will observe, such as some people act differently than others! In regard to the recommendation in the following table to "Provide oversight so that your baby is not exposed to events that could upset or overwhelm them, or content with anything intended for older children or adults," Sylvia's parents are not wrong in wanting to shelter her from ungallant behaviors exhibited by other children or adults. So too, Sylvia needs socialization and interaction with peers, not just adults. It can be a challenge for parents to meet all of the goals and Sylvia's parents might consider social experiences which incrementally add the number of children. For example, by beginning with a small library reading circle of just a few children and their caregivers, the next step might be a playdate at the park with a slightly larger group of children from a local organization such as Mothers of Preschoolers (MOPS), then Sylvia's parents might consider a larger setting again where children are riding a local carousel.

Many local libraries offer children's reading time on a regular basis, which can be beneficial in many ways for social, emotional, and language development. Local schools may also offer a home visitors' program that is available for all children from birth on to school age to help them become prepared and school ready for kindergarten. Parents can look into free resources and consider the socialization piece of the opportunity that may not be overtly stated as an element of the activity or program. If possible, parents might want to consider going to more than one library story time, such as Mondays at one library and Wednesdays at another library in the region.

Since Sylvia is somewhat shy, specific strategies to consider in Sylvia's case for home, school, and community could focus on building her interpersonal skills of social awareness and relationships with other children. To increase her social awareness and mental flexibility toward others, it will be helpful to provide play opportunities where the adults model playing together, visiting, being open to creative spontaneity, and interacting with others. Parents make important choices when hiring babysitters and selecting daycare locations for their young children. As listed in the table with parent behaviors, it is important for parents to discuss their social and emotional developmental goals with caregivers that they hire and to also discuss with their child the importance of telling their parents all about their time with others.

TABLE 3.3 Case Analysis for Sylvia

Child Name	Behavior Needs Observed	Suggested Strategies
Sylvia	• Social awareness • Relationship skills • Mental flexibility • Self-advocacy	• Playtime should include role modeling with her parents playing with others, such as grandparents, family friends, and house guests • Participation opportunities in activities and clubs such as at the children's library • Daily family story time together using books that show interactions with others. In addition to reading the words, talk about what is observed in the picture. Point to details in the pictures and ask Sylvia questions about the illustrations and what she notices • They will also want to speak with Sylvia about self-advocacy when someone is speaking to her in an unexpected way and to tell her parents at home

Toys and Activities Appropriate for Birth to Two Years of Age

The toy market for babies and toddlers can be mind-boggling with lots of soft toys, blinking plastic toys, and toys that talk and sing. Toys and activities appropriate for birth to two years of age provide many suggestions for parents and caregivers to interact with their young child. The best toys and activities are ones that provide opportunities for interaction between the child and adult to develop their socialization, language, and physical skills. Wooden toys are frequently encouraged to stimulate creativity as opposed to plastic toys with blinking lights, sound, and buttons to push. Human learning involves both failures and successes. Toys and experiences should provide children with learning opportunities to grow by experiencing both failures and successes during playtime.

When selecting activities and toys from the charts, consider whether your child is advanced enough to move to the next row

TABLE 3.4 Toys and Activities Appropriate for Birth to Two Years of Age

Age	Toys	Activities	Parent Behaviors
One to three months of age	Images or books with high contrast patterns. Bright, varied mobile. Rattles.	Singing to your baby. Playing varied music from music boxes, digital, radio, CDs, cassette tapes, and records.	
Four to seven months	Encourage your child to reach for toys. Provide baby blocks and soft toys that stimulate eye-to-hand coordination and fine motor skills.	Spend time on the floor playing with your child every day.	If your child will be cared for by others, choose quality child care that will be affectionate, responsive, educational, and safe. Visit your child care provider frequently and share your ideas about positive caregiving. Make sure that other people who provide care and supervision for your baby understand the importance of forming a loving and comforting relationship with your child.
Eight to 12 months	Stacking toys in different sizes, shapes, colors. Cups, pails, and other unbreakable containers. Unbreakable mirrors of various sizes. Bath toys that float, squirt, or hold water. Large building blocks. "Busy boxes" that push, open, squeak, and more. Squeeze toys. Large dolls and puppets. Cars, trucks, and other vehicle toys made of flexible plastic, with no sharp edges or removable parts.	Stimulating infant brain growth: Play with blocks and soft toys to develop hand-to-eye coordination, fine motor skills, and a sense of competence. Provide a stimulating, safe environment where your baby can begin to explore and roam safely. Read every day. Visit the library and check out new board books every week. Keep a record of titles read with a reading app.	Stimulating infant brain growth: Talk to your baby, using adult talk, during all activities dressing, bathing, feeding, playing, walking, driving, shopping, etc. Be attentive to your baby and respond to all of their behaviors. Baby is tuned in and will be able to read their parents faces for emotions so temper strong emotions.

Balls of all sizes, but not small enough to fit in the mouth.
Cardboard books with large pictures.
Music boxes, musical toys, and child safe music players.
Push pull toys.
Toy telephones.
Paper tubes, empty boxes, old magazines, egg cartons, empty plastic water bottles (without a lid or small cap as that could be a potential choking hazard).

Use foreign language skills at home.
Play games like peekaboo and pattycake to stimulate your baby's memory skills.
Introduce your child to other children and parents.
Teach your baby to wave "bye-bye" and to shake their head "yes" and "no."
Spend time on the floor playing with your child every day.

Give consistent warm, physical contact with hugs to establish your child's sense of security and well-being.
Provide oversight so that your baby is not exposed to events that could upset or overwhelm them, or to entertainment or media content with anything intended for older children or adults.
Continue the behaviors listed in previous months behaviors like making sure other people who provide care and supervision understand the importance of forming a loving and comforting relationship with them.
Respect your baby's periodic discomfort around people who are not primary caregivers.

(Continued)

TABLE 3.4 (Continued)

Age	Toys	Activities	Parent Behaviors
One year	To stimulate brain growth in your one-year-old: Choose toys that encourage creativity. Select simple toys and encourage your child to be imaginative with their toys. Encourage playing with blocks and soft toys. Encourage your child to look at books and draw with paper and crayons. Play with and rotate some of the following toys. Board books with large pictures, simple stories. Books and magazines with photographs of babies. Blocks and nesting toys. Simple shape sorters and pegboards. Beginner jigsaw puzzles. Toys that encourage make believe play like broom sets, etc. Digging toys, bucket, shovel, rake. Dolls of all sizes. Cars, trucks, trains. Unbreakable containers of all shapes and sizes. Bath toys – boats, containers, floating squeak toys. Balls of all shapes and sizes. Push and pull toys. Outdoor toys, like slides, swings, sandboxes. Beginner's tricycle. Connecting toys, links, large stringing beads, etc. Stuffed animals. Child keyboard and other musical instruments. Large crayons. Toy telephone. Unbreakable mirrors of various sizes. Dress up clothes. Wooden spoons, old magazines, baskets, cardboard boxes and tubes, pots and pans, other similar safe, unbreakable items she "finds" around the house.	Playing on the floor together daily and coloring. Turning over containers to pour out the contents. Building towers of four blocks or more. Develop word associations by naming everyday objects and activities. Read books daily that encourage touching and pointing to objects, and read rhymes, jingles, and nursery stories. Play fun, calm, and melodic music for your child. Listen to and answer your child's questions. Ask questions to stimulate the decision-making process. Begin to explain safety in simple terms; such as feeling the temperature of the water teaches the meaning and danger of hot things.	Understand the following: Children learn through social interactions and play. Learning happens over time in safe, stable, nourishing relationships. If a child is fearful, very little new learning will occur. Talk about upcoming activities with simple, upbeat language to prepare the child for new experiences. Give consistent, warm, physical contact with hugs to establish your toddler's sense of security and well-being. Avoid using food as a reward, but rather use verbal praise and hug your child for good behavior. Choose quality child care that is affectionate, responsive, educational, and safe.

| Two years | Age-appropriate puzzles, blocks, simple musical instruments, age appropriate vehicles like trucks and tractors, toy houses, stuffed animals, and balls. | Encourage creative play, building, and drawing. Provide time and tools for playful learning. Listen to appropriate and calm music. Continue to read together daily, be responsive to your child's needs, give warm physical contact, talk and sing to your child while doing all activities. | When you see your child starting to get worked up, try to turn his attention and energy to an activity that is more acceptable. If distraction does not work, ignore the behavior rather than reward it with extra attention. Limit and monitor screen time and viewing. |

Adapted from Shelov, 2014.

in the table. Remember that asynchronous (uneven) development is common among young gifted children, they may be ready for more advanced cognitive activities but may also need additional practice with age-level social activities.

Summary of Birth to Two Years

For all children, play is learning. Offering a variety of learning activities to play individually, with an adult, and with other children in circle time is important for the development of infants and toddlers during the first two years of life. Conventional recommendations in gifted education are to provide above-level educational opportunities that are one to two years advanced depending on the child's ability levels. Similar thinking could be applied with reading books to young children. Perhaps a two-year-old child would benefit from reading a book that is intended for three- and four-year-olds. However, when providing above-level activities, adults should be attuned to possible frustration and make adjustments appropriately. Adults must take care and not provide toys that are too advanced over a child's age level that may include choking hazards. Routinely check all toys for small parts that could be pulled or broken off. Also look for sharp edges, which can pose a danger. Do not attach a toy to a crib since the baby could pull it or become entangled in it. Never give a baby any food or small object that could cause choking. All foods should be mashed, ground, or soft enough to swallow without chewing.

Discussion Questions

Table 3.5 provides specific behavior needs that were observed in each case study and suggested strategies and possible topics that could be applied and considered with each case study. Use the questions that follow the table to further discuss the case details and how interventions could be used with the children's cases described.

Characteristics and Case Studies, Birth to Two Years ◆ 59

TABLE 3.5 Summary of Case Analyses Needs and Suggestions: Very Young Children, Birth to Two Years

Child Name	Behavior Needs Observed	Suggested Strategies
Zachary	• Self-awareness • Relationship skills • Mental flexibility	• Provide appropriate toys for baby challenge • Model and practice physical skills • Daily book reading for at least 30 minutes • Use a baby mirror to model speaking skills and emotional expressions • Model friendships with others • Model routines and problem solving
Sylvia	• Social awareness • Relationship skills • Mental flexibility • Self-advocacy	• Playtime should include role modeling with her parents playing with others, such as grandparents, family friends, and house guests • Participation opportunities in activities and clubs such as at the children's library • Daily family story time together using books that show interactions with others. In addition to reading the words, talk about what is observed in the picture. Point to details in the pictures and ask Sylvia questions about the illustrations and what she notices • The parents will also want to speak with Sylvia about ideas associated with self-advocacy so that when someone speaks to her in an unexpected way, she is prepared to tell her parents at home

1. Using the information in each case study and in the discussion table, consider the behaviors described and identify strategies that may work both at home and at school.
2. Select one of the cases and identify additional behaviors that exist in both the home and school setting. Describe how these behaviors would impact the child's interactions with others.
3. In response to the children's needs, imagine and create a supportive environment that could accommodate the children described in the case studies. What elements should be

included? What strategies and techniques could be implemented to meet their developing needs?

References

Copple, C., & Bredekamp, S. (2009). *Developmentally appropriate practice in early childhood programs serving children from birth through age 8*. National Association for the Education of Young Children.

Eisenberg, A., Murkoff, H., & Hathaway, S. (1996). *What to expect the first year.* Workman Publishing, p. 356.

Hertzog, N., & Gadzikowski, A. (2017). *Early childhood gifted education: Fostering talent development.* National Association for Gifted Children.

Jolly, J. L., & Matthews, M. S. (2012). A critique of the literature on parenting gifted learners. *Journal for the Education of the Gifted, 35*, 259–290. https://doi.org/10.1177/0162353212451703.

Jolly, J. L., Treffinger, D. J., Inman, T. F., & Smutny, J. F. (2011). *Parenting gifted children.* Prufrock Press.

Morelock, M. J. (1992). Giftedness: The view from within. *Understanding Our Gifted, 4*(3), 1, 11–15.

NAGC. (n.d.). Asynchronous development. https://www.nagc.org/resources-publications/resources-parents/social-emotional-issues/asynchronous-development.

Papadopoulos, D. (2021). Parenting the exceptional social-emotional needs of gifted and talented children: What do we know? *Children (Basel, Switzerland), 8*(11), 953. https://doi.org/10.3390/children8110953.

Robinson, N. M. (2000). Giftedness in very young children: How seriously should it be taken? In Friedman, R. C., & Shore, B. M. (Eds.), *Talents unfolding: Cognition and development* (pp. 7–26). American Psychological Association.

Shelov, S. (2014). *The complete and authoritative guide caring for your baby and young child: Birth to age 5* (6th ed.). American Academy of Pediatrics. Bantam Books.

4

Characteristics and Case Studies of Preschool Children, Ages Three To Five Years

Children ages three to five years are engaging, challenging, and love to explore. At this age they start to gain independence and develop strong personalities. This chapter will focus specifically on three children in this age range with vast personality differences and explore the application of strategies to use with different cases.

Characteristics of Three- to Five-Year-Olds

There is a great deal of growth that happens for children between the ages of three and five. All children develop skills at a different rate, however there are some specific developmental characteristics that are important for this time period between three and five years. Table 4.1 provides an overview of the specific skills and characteristics of a child between the ages of three and five.

The case studies below highlight how social emotional characteristics may look among various children. These cases highlight the children's unique social emotional maturity beyond their

DOI: 10.4324/9781003353690-4

TABLE 4.1 From Table 1.1: Developmental Trends between Ages Three and Five Years

Stages	Physical Development	Cognitive Development	Social Emotional Development
Three to five years	• Increased motor skills such as running, skipping, throwing, building. • Increased competence in basic self-care. • More mature looking physical features. • Acquisition of fine motor skills – pencil grip. • Transition away from afternoon nap.	• Dramatic play and fantasy with peers. • Ability to draw simple figures. • Acknowledge colors, letters, and numbers. • Recognition and retelling of familiar stories and events. • Reasoning that is often illogical. • Frequent self-talk. • Limited understanding of how adults typically interpret events.	• Developing understanding of gender and ethnicity. • Development of the ability to defer immediate gratification – sharing. • Modest appreciation that other people have their own desires. • Some demonstration of sympathy for people in distress.

McDevitt, T.M. & Ormrod, J.E., (2013). *Child development and education (fifth edition)*. Pearson, pp. 26–27.

developmental ages. The advanced manifestation of the developmental levels varies with each child and interacts with their cognitive and physical stages. As each case study is presented and discussed, the focus will be on the social emotional aspect and strategies that may be used for the specific child. Some strategies are beneficial for more than just the specific child described and may also be used to benefit an entire class of young learners. It is recommended to use the strategies described as broadly as possible as there may be elements that other children in the classroom will be able to connect with and practice. The three case studies in this chapter describe Sanjali, a sensitive, empathetic child; Miguel, an English language learner; and Jeriah, an energetic child. Each case study provides a description of the child highlighting the social emotional characteristics as well as a discussion of the specific case and strategies to address the social emotional characteristics.

Case Study – Sanjali

Sanjali is a four-year-old highly gifted child with a strong empathetic side. She is aware of and concerned for her preschool classmates and their feelings. She enjoys school and spending time with her friends and teachers. In the classroom, she stands back and observes her classmates as they play. When she feels comfortable, she joins them. She is well-liked by her classmates and is sought out for her playful imagination and creativity. She is compassionate with other children and often the first to reach out to a friend if they have been injured or are upset. The classroom teachers recognize her giftedness and sensitivities and try to foster her cognitive growth while supporting her sensitivities.

At the beginning of the school year, Sanjali displayed some transition issues into her new school environment. Sanjali, stood outside the classroom, did not speak to other students or adults, and was an observer, not engaging in activities. She was slow to trust her teachers, but began to flourish after several weeks in the classroom. She was able to focus on the teacher's emotions to develop a sense of authentic trust, prior to feeling comfortable in the classroom.

After about the sixth month of school, the parents of Sanjali traveled out of town for an overnight trip and her grandmother came to stay with her while her parents were gone. This arrangement had occurred before and Sanjali was aware of the plan and agenda for the evening her parents were gone. Her grandmother had been to the school before and successfully dropped Sanjali off that morning. She had a great day but, when dismissal time came, Sanjali's grandmother was not there to pick her up from school as planned.

Caught in traffic, her grandmother called the school and left a message that she would probably be 30 minutes late. After waiting for her grandmother to come, the teacher realized there was a phone message and conveyed the message to Sanjali explaining that her grandmother was on her way. Sanjali immediately started crying and was inconsolable. Sanjali's expected plan was not happening the way she thought.

With her parents gone, and her grandmother late, Sanjali was triggered by a memory of the Disney movie "Frozen." Sanjali was highly upset that Ana and Elsa's parents did not return from their trip and left them alone. Her concerns left her completely unable to move and she could not function. With no one able to comfort her, she sobbed until her grandmother arrived at the school.

When Sanjali finally saw her grandmother, she calmed down but began expressing her concern that her parents were not going to return home. After the incident, her parents returned home as promised and she resumed her "normal" routine but continued to have issues coming to school for another full week. She could not seem to move past the concern that she would be left at school and that someone would not do what they had said. Although school was a safe environment, she was still unable to function. For the next week, she spent classroom time crying or watching the clock to know exactly how much longer until dismissal, living in fear that she would not be picked up as promised.

Discussion of Sanjali's Case

Sanjali has a strong *awareness* when it comes to the responsibilities of others and also needs to develop the skill of *self-awareness* when she becomes overwhelmed with her emotions. This self-awareness can be developed through skills of *self-talk* and *identifying her emotions*. To help her understand her reaction it is beneficial for Sanjali to discuss her feelings and emotions. This can be led by an adult through discussion, drawing pictures, and using feeling cards or pictures. Allowing her to name the emotions that she feels will provide adults with a chance to talk with her about emotions as well as to develop strategies to cope with these emotions. The goal of this discussion strategy is to validate the feelings and then help create behaviors around those feelings that are more productive. For example, her father could talk to her and ask if crying every day is productive for her or for her peers and what she could do to validate feelings and not impact her peers. A teddy bear or stuffed animal that is identified as the Talking Bear might be placed in the classroom. When introduced to the classroom the Talking Bear is available to hear stories, listen to feelings, or share things that make them mad, happy, sad, etc. The focus on self-talk and identifying emotions provides children with the opportunity to share this information without being judged. Children need to be encouraged to share their feelings; however a stuffed animal may be more comfortable for them to use while they are building the relationship with others.

Sanjali's *social awareness* of her behavior and the impact on others is helpful to address. This awareness integrates with the goal setting and understanding of routines. Helping her recognize that her behavior can have a direct impact on herself and others will provide her with a stronger self-awareness as well as the social awareness and relationships to others in the classroom. This skill is advanced at this age, since developmentally the child has a self-focus. Helping teachers talk with her and point out behaviors will help with her development.

Goals need to be set to help her work through the day in terms of working with her emotions and related behaviors. These goals need to be set at the beginning so that she can easily attain these and achieve feelings of success. As she continues to improve and meet the goals, they should become increasingly more challenging. One of the goals that could be set for Sanjali is to come into the classroom and focus on circle time with the goal to not cry or ask when the school day was over during circle time. Then, new goals may be set for the next part of the school day routine.

The adults in Sanjali's life need to recognize and understand her need for consistency within her routines. Sanjali's teachers and parents should set up a routine schedule for her so that she is able to identify a set *routine*. This goal is helpful to identify transitions throughout the classroom as well as when routines need to be changed. Having the schedule reflect changes will allow for *transitional time periods*. A visual schedule can be useful for students in the classroom with and without reading ability. Using a schedule also provides the opportunity for students to realize what's next during the day. Young children may not understand lengths of time yet, therefore using a schedule provides them with a sequence of events and activities to anticipate and feel prepared.

It is also important for Sanjali to *feel safe and loved*. The adults outside of school need to demonstrate and communicate with her about safety and build her trust in terms of picking her up and being honest and trustworthy. This communication is important to share with the school, so the teachers can assure her who is picking her up for the day as well as communicate with her throughout the day. In order to help Sanjali work to address her stress, adults need to communicate with her and encourage her to talk about her emotions and feelings. Adults need to work with Sanjali and help her set goals and identify daily routines. Small goals will help her to achieve success and with the success of these goals, she will build her understanding and ability to work through various situations.

Developing Sanjali's *mental flexibility* is another way parents and teachers can support her when things do not go as planned. Working with her to develop a backup plan when things do not work out as expected and role-playing different scenarios will increase her mental flexibility by providing her with the skills needed to react to a different plan and not focus on the plan that did not happen. These scenarios develop her problem-solving abilities so that she can build her *creative and critical thinking* when focusing on different solutions. To build these skills as well as her flexibility in thinking, examples should be used that do not trigger an emotional response. For example, if the weather is bad and recess needs to be inside instead of outside, ask Sanjali to think of some fun inside games to play together. This will build the skills as well as provide some comfort when things do not work as planned. As this skill becomes more comfortable, then she can be presented with harder more emotional scenarios.

Working with all children and especially Sanjali to develop a *growth mindset* is very helpful. The case demonstrated her use of a fixed mindset with negative thinking. Teaching a growth mindset with positive terminology would be more beneficial for learning how to cope with unexpected changes. For example, when something doesn't work out, using the saying "yes and…" can help develop more positive thinking. This could be, "Yes and while you wait for grandmother to come, you may spend more time putting puzzles together." This approach can be used to help guide the "no" answers and use a creative thinking approach.

Sanjali and her teachers need to continue working on these skills and *develop a long-term strategy* for addressing challenges when things do not go as planned for her. As she becomes more comfortable with developing these skills, providing *opportunities to change* the routine, use the backup plan, and create and establish new routines and transitions will help the development. Throughout the growth, it is important NOT to minimize her emotions as children's feelings are real to them. Skills that should be developed include what to do when she feels these emotions to minimize the impact of her behavior on herself and on others.

Case Study – Miguel

Miguel is a three-year-old native Spanish speaker. When he was two years old, he and his parents moved to the

United States from South America. Miguel has been introduced to English both inside and outside of the home during the year he has been in the United States but he has limited use of the English language. He began learning English in preschool and his receptive language skills developed quickly as he was able to understand and recognize nonverbal interactions and cues from his teacher and peers; however, his expressive language, the ability to produce English, is still emerging and Miguel struggles in English-only conversations. He is an empathetic and passionate child. Miguel is able to read facial expressions and interacts appropriately with peers. He plays with his peers on the playground and is very affectionate. He demonstrates high-level skills with puzzles, block design, and patterns. His mathematical thinking is advanced for his age.

During play time, Miguel builds structures with blocks and engages in imaginative, make-believe dramatic play with other students. He enjoys role-playing in the play kitchen and with cars and trucks, especially when there is limited language needed. He focuses on scenarios that include routine activities such as going to the doctor, school, or cooking. He draws other children and adults into the activity by nonverbal expressions as well as handing the individual an object to engage them in the scenario. While acting out a cooking scenario, Miguel handed a pot and a plastic food item to a classmate who was watching and then engaged her in the scenario through his interactions with her. Miguel is aware of other students in the classroom and he will purposefully include them in an activity when he notices that they are alone.

Although Miguel and his peers enjoy playing, they become frustrated with one another when they cannot understand each other verbally. Miguel becomes exasperated with his inability to communicate in English clearly with these peers in various situations. When he becomes excited or frustrated, it also becomes more difficult for him to communicate with the English language being

Characteristics and Case Studies of Preschool Children ◆ 69

learned. When this happens, he tends to become physical in order to communicate. This behavior is often viewed by his teachers and peers as aggressive and maladaptive because it sometimes involves hitting or pulling on other students to get their attention.

With the use of an English to Spanish translator, Miguel's parents are able to explain that he believes he is friends with everyone and will often report the various interactions and his concerns for every child in class when he arrives home. He worries if there is something that is perceived as unfair or unjust. His social awareness of others and empathy towards others is a characteristic that he demonstrates daily. Miguel is conscious of his own differences and sometimes becomes frustrated when his classmates do not understand him.

Discussion of Miguel's Case

Classroom activities to support Miguel should focus on discussing emotions and recognitions of emotions. Students should be able to identify these emotions as well as how to recognize behaviors that can happen when feeling these emotions. By using role-modeling and various *role-playing scenarios*, teachers and students may practice acting out various situations. This pretend role-play will provide students with the opportunities to see what behaviors look like from another person's perspective and when they are not in the middle of the specific situation. Throughout various scenarios, *critical and creative thinking* should be cultivated with specific prompts which will help children begin to understand how to develop alternative ways to act out the scenario or solve the problem. Guided reflection and discussion will provide flexibility in thinking around various ways to act in the situations. These creative thinking skills will also provide the fluency of ideas, actions, and behaviors that could be used with this scenario.

We can recognize that Miguel is very aware of what is happening in the classroom and has a strong self-awareness as well as a *social awareness* of other children. Helping him understand the actions of behaviors through *play and creative activities* will allow his communication skills to develop. Since he is able to understand nonverbal communication and demonstrates empathy, the activities he participates in will continue to enhance these skills. The use of *role-play* will continue to *boost his nonverbal communication* skills and behaviors as well as increase his awareness across activities.

Addressing *relationship skills* by discussing *impulse control* is another way to help resolve conflict. The understanding and use of various ways to communicate will provide classmates with alternatives to verbal language. Teaching impulse control can be modeled through the use of *play* including various activities within the environment. The use of play-based communication activities such as miming and charades will help students understand the needs of clear actions and help them develop an *awareness of intention*. As children act out words, actions, emotions, and scenarios, they will enhance and develop mindfulness of body control, use of their body to communicate, and nonverbal communication skills. These activities can be pulled from and reinforced as students work through their own challenging scenarios during play.

The classroom teachers need to continue to build a safe environment for Miguel through a specific focus on *celebrating cultural diversity* as well as encouraging various ways to communicate. *Friendship* building and various grouping activities will provide Miguel and others the opportunity to play and work with a variety of children in the classroom. Specific grouping around passions and interests will be beneficial for all of the children and especially for Miguel as he is looking to continue building communication skills. His classmates may be taught familiar Spanish words to enhance communication with Miguel. Centers should be labeled in both English and Spanish to celebrate diversity and value all members within the classroom.

Miguel's communication skills in English will continue to develop. Using sentence stems and images for emotions will help him communicate and can be scaffolded so he has both the Spanish and English terms. He needs support and understanding to continue to develop these skills while learning to communicate in various ways. His behavior is a result of frustration around the communication; therefore, skills related to nonverbal communication will reduce his frustration until his English communication skills develop. Miguel's long-term *goal* is to enhance his verbal communication skills and continued support will be needed both inside and outside the home. Respecting various forms of communication will be critical for Miguel and his classmates.

Case Study – Jeriah

Jeriah is an enthusiastic highly verbal four-year-old gifted learner, and he enjoys coming to school to converse with his teachers and peers. During these conversations, he becomes so excited and focused on a topic that he dominates the conversation and controls the pace of the discussion. Often when asked questions about his topic, Jeriah appears not to hear the questions, chooses not to answer, or asks for them to be repeated. When this happens, his peers and his teachers have, at times, become frustrated. Jeriah loves learning and often because of his excitement to learn has a difficult time staying focused on the specific task at hand. He wants to learn many things at once and becomes easily bored with routine tasks. Jeriah loves to move and enjoys centers where he can move such as block building, imaginary play, and the sensory table. He is physically active, energetic, and liked by his friends. He is empathetic to his classmates and his teachers, making sure he connects with them each day on a personal level.

During center time, Jeriah moves from center to center and has a difficult time completing a specific task but prefers to try a little bit of everything. When asked what his favorite centers are, he will tell the teacher, "All of them." When adults provide him with verbal directions, he only picks up on various elements within the directions and appears to lose interest and tune out part way through the directions. At classroom centers, an adult is needed to sit with him to complete a task in order to provide him the directions in small step-by-step increments.

Teachers have talked with his parent and discovered that he exhibits similar behavior at home related to task completion. He is often able to use his verbal skills to talk himself out of a task, only completing part of the task or convincing his older siblings to complete it for him. He is able to avoid consequences for not completing tasks because he is able to connect with the person making the request.

Discussion of Jeriah's Case

Since Jeriah is highly verbal his teachers are able to sit with him and talk through his inability to complete tasks. *Relationship building* is important for Jeriah and discussion helps him acknowledge his physical movement around the classroom and his lack of task completion, and task persistence. The verbal discussion provides him the opportunity for *self-talk* and *self-awareness*. Teachers guide him through his reflections on his energy level in the classroom related to his movement around the space and the effect it has on other classmates. Discussion around his *emotions* and his feelings during center time is beneficial to the teacher in order to acknowledge his perception of events and encourage him to focus on task persistence and task completion.

During class, teachers work with Jeriah to organize and plan his time at centers. This plan includes a focus on *impulse control* providing him a focus to identify and avoid the behavior that is distracting him and others from completion of the tasks. Each day he is given a specific task list with a *goal* of what to complete at each center. The teacher explains to Jeriah each task and all the steps needed to complete the task. Each center has directions, using both images and simple vocabulary, that provide him with the previously explained steps to complete the task. These directions, as well as a specific checklist or menu of tasks, will help guide him during the center time. During class, the teachers can spend time communicating with him and checking in to make sure he understands the task, is making progress in completing elements, and is *persistent* in working on the goal.

For Jeriah, continued development of persistence and task completion is important to focus on the long-term development. In thinking about his needs, it is critical to help figure out the purpose of the task avoidance. The reason behind the non-completion is important to identify as it may signal a lack of interest in the center topics or specific skills that need to be addressed. With the use of the executive functioning skills, detailed instructions, focus on specific tasks, enhanced open communication, and developed awareness about his behavior, Jeriah will continued to develop the specific skills needed for *self-management*.

Summary

Children between the ages of three and five years demonstrate various characteristics and needs at developmental levels. It is important when working with children to understand their individual development as well as their individual needs, communicate with all adults, and use tools to help children understand and continue to develop. Working with families is critical in the process of supporting young children. Specific tools and strategies such as these discussed within these three cases can be used at home and school.

Sanjali, Miguel, and Jeriah are unique individuals with a range of social emotional concerns and challenges. Their social emotional behaviors impact their daily classroom and home environments and should be addressed in order for the child to be ready for high-level, engaging content and curricular experiences. Children will become independent learners when compassionate adults use a combination of developmentally appropriate skills and a variety of strategies.

74 ◆ Characteristics and Case Studies of Preschool Children

TABLE 4.2 Summary of Case Analyses Needs and Suggestions: Preschool Children, Ages Three to Five Years

Child Name	Behavior Observed	Suggested Strategies
Sanjali	• Self-awareness • Social awareness • Mental flexibility • Growth mindset	• Self-talk and identifying her emotions and using a Talking Bear • Establish and follow routines and set small attainable goals • Use creative and critical thinking skills to create a Plan B • Continue positive talk
Miguel	• Social awareness of others and empathy • Critical and creative thinking • Awareness of attention • Celebrating cultural diversity • Friendship skill building • Goal setting	• Role-playing scenarios • Provide experiences through play and creative activities • Use mindfulness techniques • Communication activities and role-playing • Grouping strategies • Focus on short- and long-term attainable goals to build communication skills
Jeriah	• Relationship building • Self-talk and self-awareness • Impulse control • Self-management	• Discussion with an adult • Self-talk and identifying emotions with a trusted adult • Goal setting and persistence of task • Skills taught in the area of executive functioning, time management, step-by-step directions, and enhanced communication

Discussion Questions

Table 4.2 provides specific topics that were discussed in each case study.

1. Using the information in each case study and in the discussion table, compare and contrast the behaviors identified among the various cases as well as the suggested strategies.

2. Select either Sanjali, Miguel, or Jeriah's case and identify additional behaviors that exist as well as additional strategies that could be implemented.
3. Think through each case and create a classroom environment that could accommodate all three of these children. What elements should be included? What strategies and techniques could be implemented to meet all of their needs?

5

Characteristics and Case Studies of School-Age Children, Ages Six to Eight Years

Children that range in ages from six to eight are in the primary grades in elementary school, generally late kindergarten to second grade. Children are striving toward independence and developing understanding of peer relationships. Within this two-year span, there may be significant social and emotional, cognitive, and even physical differences between advanced children. Some of these differences are visible, while others may not present themselves immediately or at all.

Characteristics of Six- to Eight-Year-Old Children

The child's social and emotional development at this age focuses upon increasing awareness of how one's own abilities compare with peers, desire for time with friends, increasing ability to have responsibilities such as chores, adherence to rules of games, and understanding of basic moral principles (fairness and equity).

As children move through the early developmental stages, skills continue to build upon one another, and gifted characteristics begin to reveal as an overlay. Some gifted children may

DOI: 10.4324/9781003353690-5

TABLE 5.1 From Table 1.1: Developmental Trends between Ages Six and Eight Years (McDevitt & Ormrod, 2013, pp. 26–27)

Stages	Physical Development	Cognitive Development	Social Emotional Development
Six to eight years	• Successful imitations of complex physical movements – ability to ride a bicycle. • Participation in organized sports. • Steady gains in height and weight. • Refinement of gross motor skills. • Loss and replacement of primary teeth.	• Development of basic skills in reading, writing, math, and other academic subject areas. • Ability to reason logically about concrete objects and events in the immediate environment.	• Increasing awareness of how one's own abilities compare with peers. • Desire for time with age-mates. • Increasing ability to have responsibilities such as chores. • Adherence to rules of games. • Understanding of basic moral principles (fairness and equity).

progress through the developmental stages and acquire given skills at a faster pace than the average student. It is important to recognize that there may be a vast difference in skills due to interest, socio-economic, and cultural background as well as previous experiences.

According to Barbara Clark (2013), there are four functions of the brain where gifted characteristics emerge. These include the cognitive function (linear and spatial), affective function (emotional and social), physical function (sensing and movement), and the intuitive function. While characteristics of giftedness are seen throughout all four areas, the focus of this chapter is specifically on the affective function. While research varies as to the degree or level in which the characteristics interact and affect growth, "gifted learners show characteristics different from their age peers in each of the areas of function, although all gifted individuals have their own unique patterns of characteristics and no gifted learner exhibits every characteristic in every area" (Clark, 1992, p. 37).

Affective characteristics of gifted children may include unusual sensitivity to the expectations and feelings of others;

78 ◆ Characteristics and Case Studies of School-Age Children

a feeling of being different; idealism and a sense of justice; unusual emotional depth and intensity. Affective characteristics specifically may look and be valued very differently across a wide variety of cultures. Cultures that are based in more of a collectivist approach tend to value the group over the individual. Characteristics that tend to be more focused on the group include unusual emotional depth and intensity, strong level of empathy, and capacity for conceptualizing and solving societal and environmental problems. This is important to understand since often schools tend to support the white dominant characteristics that are more individualistic such as high levels of frustration with self, heightened self-awareness, and a strong need for consistency between abstract values and personal actions. Culture plays an important factor in the characteristics that are valued both in and out of the home. These characteristics merge with the child's developmental level and cultural values. As each child is different, a particular gifted child might exhibit some or all of the characteristics within Table 5.2: Affective Characteristics of Giftedness (Clark, 2013).

Understanding affective characteristics and social emotional development are important when designing programming and interacting with young gifted learners. The traditional developmental levels may be inconsistent when a six-year-old cognitively functions at an eight-year-old level while emotionally functions at a three-year-old level. It is also important to recognize that

TABLE 5.2 Affective Characteristics of Giftedness (Clark, 2013)

• Unusual sensitivity to the expectations and feelings of others	• Strong need for consistency between abstract values and personal actions
• Heightened self-awareness, accompanied by a feeling of being different	• Advanced levels of moral judgment
• Idealism and sense of justice	• Advanced cognitive and affective capacity for conceptualizing and solving societal problems
• High expectations of self and others, often leading to high levels of frustration with self, others, and situations; perfectionism	• Ability to develop solutions to social and environmental problems
	• Earlier development of inner locus of control
	• Unusual emotional depth and intensity

children living in physically or emotionally unsafe environments or who do not have emotional stability may display characteristics at a different level.

When addressing the unique social and emotional needs of gifted learners, developmental and affective characteristics should be considered. The interconnectedness of characteristics is important when working with young gifted children as their development is asynchronous – really high in some areas and average or lower in others. Silverman (1993) explained that "giftedness has an emotional as well as a cognitive substructure: cognitive complexity gives rise to emotional depth. Thus, gifted children not only *think* differently from their peers, they also *feel* differently" (p. 3). The case studies presented in this chapter offer insight into a few examples of how these characteristics and developmental traits manifest in some children. While there are often many areas that a child can work on, the adults need to help focus on the most meaningful strategies and skills for that time period. Children grow and change so fast that it is important to remember that the challenges of today may not necessarily be the challenges of tomorrow.

Identification of Giftedness

The United States Department of Education has no laws or mandates related to identification or programming of gifted children. Therefore each state is allowed to create and enforce their own procedures, definitions, mandates, and laws. This leads to a range of procedures, programming, funding, and training around giftedness. According to the National Association for Gifted Children Position Statement approved in 2019, "Students with gifts and talents perform—or have the capability to perform—at higher levels compared to others of the same age, experience, and environment in one or more domains. They require modification(s) to their educational experience(s) to learn and realize their potential." As a leading organization for giftedness, there are also recommendations for how to identify children from all racial, ethnic, and cultural populations as well as economic strata. Understanding and using a wide range of tools in order to identify and program for gifted learners is critical in addressing the inequities within gifted education programming.

As young elementary children approach the eligible age for school gifted programs, it is useful for parents and families to understand what children are evaluated upon to be identified for participation in school gifted programs. There are several areas within giftedness that can be identified. Table 5.3: Areas of Giftedness Identification provides some general information and definitions about general intellectual ability, and specific academic or talent aptitudes. Identification protocols for gifted programming eligibility vary among state, local education agencies, and programmatic purposes and goals.

TABLE 5.3 Areas of Giftedness Identification

Area of Giftedness Identification	Explanation
General Intellectual Ability	General intellectual ability does not necessarily translate to a specific academic area. This is an overall identification without a specific content area. Students identified here may be quick to grasp concepts, make connections, or display other general characteristics.
Specific Academic Aptitude	This area of identification is mostly related to mathematics and English language arts. Some schools and districts identify students with strengths in areas of social studies, sciences, and/or world language. If there is a gifted program, generally math and language arts is supportive; however depending on the support, it is possible that only one or several of the academic areas are supported.
Specific Talent Aptitude	Identification in this area may include areas such as arts, creativity, dance, music, leadership, and psychomotor. While these areas are often included in identification, the programming within schools may not be supported. If schools have a gifted program, it is most often in the areas of academics.

Adapted from Papadopoulos, D. (2021).

For information about specific identification and programming services, it is recommended to look at the state department of education and school district that the child attends or will be attending. Connecting with organizations may be beneficial for general information and advocacy tools.

Case Study – Zuri

Zuri is a six-year-old social child who finds joy in spending time and talking with others. She has many friends on the playground and makes an effort to include other classmates that are alone on the playground or at lunch. Zuri is not a strong test taker and often scores lower on district-level tests and curriculum-based measures than she does on her daily work or with differentiated demonstrations of performance. Most recently, she participated in her district's online universal kindergarten screening for gifted classes; and while her scores were higher than the majority of her classmates, they were not high enough to meet the requirements for placement in her district's gifted program.

Her family is very religious and spends the majority of their time outside of school at church. Zuri is able to read, cite, and memorize scripture with appropriate context for the situation. At school, she demonstrates strong reading ability however her teacher tested her at grade level. Zuri does not challenge the teacher's assumption and at school only reads what is provided to her. The family is very supportive of Zuri and when asked about programming placement, the GT teacher and classroom teacher confirmed that she is getting enough challenges in the regular classroom.

Zuri has a remarkable speaking presence and at church is often asked to assist with the sermon. Her faith is very important to the family as is the collaboration and support of others. She loves other students and adults and is a natural leader. Zuri has a strong sense of social justice and encourages others to do the right thing. Her ability to connect to peers and adults provides her the ability to fit into any social context.

When Zuri's family attends teacher conferences, they are surprised by the average work that the teacher shows them. They talk with the teacher and share that Zuri is reading chapter books at home and working on much higher-level math. The teacher is surprised to hear that and reinforces that she is right at grade level where her peers in class are performing. The family is concerned but does not want to challenge the teacher out of respect for her position.

Discussion of Zuri's Case

Zuri tends to be a teacher pleaser at school. She demonstrates respect for the teacher and does not challenge the teacher's belief about her and her work level. When thinking through the social emotional skills, building *self-awareness skills* for Zuri will be beneficial. The *self-awareness* competency as defined by the Collaborative of Academic and Social Emotional Learning (CASEL) includes "capacity to recognize one's strengths and limitations with a well-grounded sense of confidence and purpose" (https://casel.org/fundamentals-of-sel/what-is-the-casel-framework/#self-awareness).

Understanding and providing her with a safe place to demonstrate her skills and strengths is important as Zuri continues to grow. She needs to be *academically challenged* so that she continues to develop her higher-level or above average skills. Encouraging her to *advocate* for herself will be important for her as she continues to grow. Advocacy looks a bit different for all individuals and for Zuri, providing her with a *mentor* or trusted adult to talk about the academic work will be helpful. This mentor can *model and practice* conversations about increasing her academic work level.

Using *bibliotherapy* specifically for topics of *self-advocacy* is a classroom and home strategy that can be utilized. Books such as *Jaime's Class Has Something to Say* by Afsaneh Moradian, *Speak Up for Yourself: A Story Teaching Children Self Advocacy* by Bryan Smith, and *How to Take the Groan out of Grown Ups* by Eric Braun can be used to demonstrate various ways that the characters talk and advocate for themselves. While the specific examples may not be the same, talking with Zuri about other situations that the skills apply to will help build her skills and comfort.

Helping Zuri develop *relationship skills* using her *leadership and speaking skills* in the classroom around academic content may be an impactful way to help her recognize her academic skills and to help the teacher see her real strengths. Through *conversation* with the family it is important that this talent area is identified in the classroom. *Communication* between the school and family is critical to help Zuri be appropriately challenged in the classroom. Tutt (2021) identified several strategies for teachers and schools to build teacher and parent communication. These include having parents and/or caregivers complete a survey about their child including attitudes, motivations, and feelings, establishing two-way communication to focus on social emotional and academic learning and events from school and home, have the families come into the classroom to share their talents, experiences, and skills, and closing the communication gap making sure that materials are sent home in native languages. Schools need to foster family and school communication in order to know the children and to understand aspects of their culture. The better the communication is with the family the more support the child will have across the environments.

In the book *Families & Educators Together: Building Great Relationships that Support Young Children* (Koralek et al., 2019) strategies and examples of family engagement activities are shared. Items such as hosting a coffee every Friday, recruiting involvement from families for events, activities, and socials, understanding, collaborating, and partnering with the community and neighborhood the students come from, are examples and elements that are shared with specific details. Regardless of the resource and strategy, one of the best ways to support young learners is through family and school collaboration and communication!

Case Study – Veer

Veer is highly talented at taking apart and repairing mechanical workings. As a seven-year-old first-grade student, he is best at science and math. He is advanced and some of his teachers often don't know what to do especially since he grasps the principles they are teaching almost before they can finish describing the ideas. Veer is able to complete assignments quickly. During the second half of the year, he has started to only partially pay attention during class. This has caused situations where he makes incorrect connections or assumptions about the content. These situations become challenging because he believes he knows the answer or content and does not take time to correct his misunderstanding.

When he thinks that something needs to be accomplished, he does so by himself. He likes to read and when topics are presented to him that he does not know as much about, he researches the topic and learns what he can quickly. During group work, in the classroom he may become quiet while he assesses the capabilities and knowledge levels of those around him. He becomes indignant when his group members are not working as quickly or in the same manner that he is and has to wait for his peers to catch up to what he is doing.

Veer enjoys being a leader outside of the classroom; however he becomes frustrated when he needs to repeat himself because others are not listening. He is sensitive to his peers and works to include everyone in games and pretend play but he is insensitive to his peers' academic work. He loves to talk about bicycles and transportation-related topics including repairing his bicycle and mapping out various routes to the stores. He likes to organize bike rides with his friends to try out new trails and routes.

Discussion of Veer's Case

At school, Veer needs to be provided with high-level content across content areas. He needs to be challenged to learn and apply new skills making sure the lessons are differentiated for him. Teachers should work to develop a *strong relationship* with Veer in order to help build his *self-awareness* around content knowledge. Working with Veer to set *goals around his learning* and the content that will be covered will help him understand the depth and breadth of content. The goals can include connecting new content with skills and knowledge that he has already attained. It is important for Veer to develop skills to maintain focus in class and recognize when he is starting to become distracted. *Higher-level content or activities* should help his focus and identifying strategies to help maintain focus is important as well. Strategies may include identifying a real-world connection to the content, a fidget item such as a stress ball, or a subtle signal from the teacher to redirect his focus.

For group work and interactions with others, he should increase his skills and strategies in the areas of *social awareness* and *relationship skills*. One technique to help him become better in group work settings is to develop his *mental flexibility*. He needs to practice various ways to *solve problems*. An activity to help with this is to provide a challenge to play a game with a different set of rules. An individual activity would be to do a maze but instead of beginning at the start, he actually begins at the end. Class or small group activities to help build include exploring logic problems, spatial reasoning activities, math puzzles, and focus activities. When playing a game, the winner could be predetermined, taking the competition out of the event, but challenging the players to figure out how to let the selected person win.

For experience and practice working in groups without one way of solving the problem or identifying an answer, the classroom should use either or both *project-based learning* and/or *problem-based learning*. Project-based learning focuses on the outcome of a real-world final project and problem-based learning focuses on having the group create a solution to the problem presented. Provide opportunities for Veer to *work in groups* using creative problem solving with open-ended answers. When selecting groups, students should have various roles and understand the strengths needed for each role. Roles might include a recorder, a writer, an artist, a mathematician, and other roles specific for the project. This type of group will assist Veer in recognizing the strengths of the additional group members.

Role-play activities that focus on tolerance and respect of others will be helpful for Veer. These scenarios can take place both at

86 ◆ Characteristics and Case Studies of School-Age Children

home and in school. He could also benefit from role-play activities that focus on tolerance.

Case Study – Margaret

Margaret is eight years old and lives in a small Midwestern town. While scoring high on standardized tests, she has not been identified for a gifted program. Teachers praise her for being sweet, responsible, quiet, and helpful. She is quick and earns high marks on every assignment. Her parents are both teachers, involved in the school, and respected among the community. She "reads" people well and began to read books as soon as she entered kindergarten. She did not want to be different so she listened quietly as the teacher taught the various letters to her. She liked to read to the class when the kindergarten teacher allowed her to do so during storybook time but was astonished when the other children did not like that she could read to them and told her that she was showing off. She soon quit reading to the group but enjoyed spelling long words backward to her family. In small groups, she took the lead for completing tasks but ceased doing so when other children told her that she was bossy. While she could count to 1,000 in kindergarten, she stopped counting at 100 when taking a numerical test since she thought the rest was repetition and that the test examiner should know them.

In first grade, she showed a good sense of humor and musical talent and enjoyed playing the lead in the class play. Margaret continued to read on her own but began getting bored with the repetition of the curriculum. She was originally in the highest math group but when she was the only girl and none of her friends was in the group, started to do poorly so she could move into a group with her friends. Her first-grade teacher did not interact with her as much as she would have liked so she began telling stories to gain her attention. Margaret's storytelling started to provide her a great deal of attention but some of her peers were hesitant to join in with the fantastical storytelling because they thought it was "lying."

In second grade, her storytelling interests were reignited when her teacher taught classical poetry, historical research, and essay writing. Margaret enjoys opportunities to perform whether with poetry recitation, reading aloud, dancing, or singing. She escapes the mundane repetition of class by reading fiction. While Margaret frequently picks biographical selections at the library, she needs specific direction with a bibliotherapy list of more sophisticated reading selections pitched above her reading level.

Margaret is a keen observer of her classmates and older students. She is very in tune and sensitive to messages about ability differences among girls and boys. She notices that the boys tend to enjoy doing math and building whereas the girls tend to participate in pretend play, writing, and reading. She stopped participating in the math and building activities because she did not want to be teased.

Discussion of Margaret's Case

Margaret can benefit from developing her *self-awareness skills* specifically in the area of recognition that she can continue to learn. While she continues to work within the classroom curriculum, she needs to be encouraged to develop her advanced skills and openness to learning. At school the material should continue to introduce high-level concepts. Introducing coping strategies such as "the power of yet" helps to focus on that a skill has not been learned yet but will be in the future and reduces negative self-talk.

Developing Margaret's *social awareness* will be important since she likes to tell stories. Understanding exaggerations and lies and the impact on relationships with others will help her recognize the implications. Using *bibliotherapy* about characters that exaggerate or lie can be helpful for her to apply the learning. Books such as *Lying Up a Storm* by Julia Cook or *I Didn't Do It* by

Sue Graves provide characters that understand the importance of telling the truth and strategies to help Margaret.

Margaret should be encouraged to *participate in clubs and activities* both in and outside of the school setting. Clubs should focus on her areas of interest that bridge the gap across content and gender. It may be helpful to find some clubs that encourage creativity in math and building such as Destination Imagination, STEAM/STEM for Girls, Lego Robotic League, MENSA, and math competitions. *Mental flexibility* can be increased by *reading biographies* of women in science, technology, engineering, arts, and math and will provide Margaret with role models and success stories. The Academy of Achievement supports a website (https://achievement.org/) that includes biographies from diverse subject and content areas as well as locations across the globe. A unique element of the website is the "find my role model" generator page where the user can input interests, personality characteristics, and challenges.

Summary

Zuri, Veer, and Margaret provide a range of children ages six to eight and represent a range of children's affective needs at the various age levels. Each child manifests developmental and social emotional characteristics in various ways. The characteristics presented with the students may be familiar to the home or school setting. Since every child is unique, they may react differently in various situations. The strategies may work well as written or need to be modified for the child's personality and the specific setting. Collaboration with the child's family is critical to make sure there is consistency across home and school connections.

Discussion Questions

Table 5.4 provides specific topics that were discussed in each case study.

Characteristics and Case Studies of School-Age Children ◆ 89

TABLE 5.4 Summary of Case Analyses Needs and Suggestions: School-Age Children, Ages Six to Eight Years

Child Name	Behavior Observed	Suggested Strategies
Zuri	• Self-awareness • Self-advocacy • Relationship skills	• Provide high-level academic challenge • Model and practice skills • Mentor • Bibliotherapy • Leadership and speaking skills • Communication
Veer	• Self-awareness • Relationship skills	• Goal setting • Provide high-level academic challenge • Mental flexibility • Problem solving • Project-based learning • Problem-based learning • Group work • Role-playing
Margaret	• Self-awareness • Social awareness • Mental flexibility	• Self-talk using the "power of yet" • Bibliotherapy • Participating in clubs and activities • Reading biographies

1. Using the information in each case study and in the discussion table, consider the behaviors described and identify strategies that may work both at home and at school.
2. Select one of the cases and identify additional behaviors that exist in both the home and school setting. Describe how these behaviors would impact the child's interactions with others.
3. In response to the children's needs, imagine and create a supportive environment that could accommodate the children described in the case studies. What elements should be included? What strategies and techniques could be implemented to meet their developing needs?

References

Collaborative for Academic and Social Emotional Learning (2020). What is the CASEL framework? https://casel.org/fundamentals-of-sel/what-is-the-casel-framework/ retrieved 6/2/22.

Clark, B. (1992). *Growing up gifted* (4th ed.). Macmillan Publishing.

Clark, B. (2013). *Growing up gifted: Developing the potential of children at home and at school* (8th ed.). Pearson Education South A.

Koralek, D., Nemeth, K., & Ramsey, K. (2019). *Families & educators together: Building great relationships that support young children.* National Association for the Education of Young Children.

Papadopoulos, D. (2021). Parenting the exceptional social-emotional needs of gifted and talented children: What do we know? *Children (Basel), 8*(11), 953. https://doi.org/10.3390/children8110953.

Silverman, L. (1993). *Counseling the gifted and talented.* Love.

Tutt, P. (2021). Teacher-parent communication strategies to start the year off right. https://www.edutopia.org/article/teacher-parent-communication-strategies-start-year-right.

6

Conclusion

Throughout these chapters, we have discussed developmental characteristics in early childhood and signs to look for advanced capabilities in young children. In review of these characteristics, it is important for parents, educators, and caretakers to remember that interaction with the environment begins to affect the infant significantly during the prenatal period and continues in subsequent years.

Review of Early Childhood Developmental Characteristics

Research has uncovered fetal abilities to hear, sense, feel, and express facial expressions prior to birth. The first three months of postnatal life may be the most critical for the infant's developing brain since the first trimester of intrauterine fetal life (Clark, 2013). Since the baby has no mobility yet, the child depends on the caregiver for all intellectual stimulation. In too many cases for the highly sensitive child, interaction may be too limited. To make sure that this period is not the greatest deprivation period for infants who are ready to interact and learn, parenting must be flexible and tailored to each infant. By providing a responsive learning environment, a parent or caregiver can respond sensitively to the child, thus providing growth and enjoyment with early learning and social interaction.

DOI: 10.4324/9781003353690-6

At eight weeks of age, infants have a capacity for interaction and begin to smile, vocalize, and hold eye contact. By three months of age, they begin to show animation toward others and feelings such as curiosity, pleasure, assertiveness, and anger. These interactions begin to establish the patterns of healthy socialization. Fun play, spontaneity, and affection provide a basis for infants to develop into trusting, loving, warm human beings. Inner locus of control develops early and how caregivers respond to the infant influences a child's personal belief that their behavior can affect the environment and that they have a role in the environment around them (Clark, 2013).

Throughout early childhood, learning experiences with other children are important in providing experiences to develop personally, socially, intellectually, and cognitively. Young children with advanced capabilities are often highly verbal with large vocabularies and some learn to read spontaneously. Others are highly interested in specific topics and actively seek information about these topics. Some parents recognize the advanced abilities and the maturity of their young children. Others may take these interests and abilities for granted, not realizing how unique these characteristics are among children (Hollingsworth, 2009).

Early identification of talent potential and access to quality programming and information is essential since parents/caregivers seem to be the best identifiers. Occasionally a teacher of preschool students will recognize exceptionally advanced abilities in a young child and talk with the parents about the possibility of having the child enter kindergarten at an early age. Early entrance to kindergarten may be a good choice for some gifted children but not all, since multiple critical factors should be considered including intellectual, social, and emotional maturity. Families may find a school willing to make an early entrance to kindergarten but many schools are opposed to early admission. It is important for parents to be aware of the advanced abilities and interests of their children so that they can begin to gather information about available accommodation options such as acceleration. Families can organize play opportunities for children to socially interact with others and respond to one another in different settings.

Importance of Social and Emotional Learning

With asynchronous development, high levels of developed cognitive ability do not guarantee high levels of affective or emotional development and vice versa. Affective learning experiences may exist naturally but opportunities to develop them must be made part of the planned growth experiences for young children. An intense sense of justice and idealism, along with self-confidence and independence are traits that can be nurtured with realistic goal setting. Unrealistic goal setting can result in feelings of frustration and inadequacy, providing a basis for future perfectionism or underachieving outcomes. Planning activities that are pitched with appropriate challenge levels for a child has been found to engage learners by supporting their intellectual needs, curiosity, and imagination.

Providing young gifted children with outlets to explore, show concern for others, persist, and grow toward mastery and challenge will nurture an early locus of control and self-efficacy in their belief to accomplish and make an impact with those around them. Social emotional well-being and adjustment among very young gifted children can be confusing in comparison with same-age peers. By thinking and planning for early affective learning experiences, children can develop personal understanding and empathy toward others to live an inspired and harmonious life.

Selecting and Using Developmentally Appropriate Strategies

As discussed within each of the chapters, when selecting developmentally appropriate strategies and learning toys, books, and materials for children, caretakers must carefully consider the child's developmental milestones, advanced behaviors displayed, and methodically select strategies that are a good fit for where the child is currently and what needs should be focused upon as

94 ◆ Conclusion

demonstrated by their behaviors. To review the CASEL competencies (self-awareness, self-management, social awareness, relationship skills, and responsible decision-making) and relate the five social emotional learning goals to activities at specific ages, consider the following suggestions and when to use them with advanced young children who may display signs of asynchronous development.

Birth to Two Years of Age

Young children are learning about their caretakers and their environments as they develop trust and comfort in others and their surroundings. Many ideas were discussed in Chapter 2. Children benefit from hearing their names. Parents and educators should integrate children's names into songs, nursery rhymes, and storybooks by substituting character names with a child's name. The Patty Cake song is a nice example, instead of singing B for Baby, sing the child's initial and name. Songs such as "Where is [baby's name]? repeat, Here she is! We are glad you're here! Sing and play, sing and play" (sung to the tune of Frère Jacques).

To develop *self-awareness* among very young children, consider what kinds of verbal feedback the child receives. Throughout the day, babies and toddlers should be part of the conversations that are occurring and actively included in the dialogue that happens between other family members. Using appealing word choice and rich vocabulary helps to create more brain connections and expand a baby's listening and observing world. Using baby mirrors to observe word formation assists with language development and can also support interactive games between the child and their parent.

Self-management activities may include providing choices between what clothes the child will wear and what activities to do next. For example, on a hot day when the air conditioner is on cold, inside, a child may want to wear their coat, but if headed outside, two clothing choices appropriate for the outside temperature could be offered for the child to select from, along with an ongoing conversation about temperature vocabulary, weather, seasons, and how the temperature makes us feel.

Children build their *social awareness* by observing others. If they observe others yell across a room, then that is what they would expect. But, if they are approached with a polite greeting before beginning a conversation about what "we" are going to do today and tomorrow, then children appreciate knowing what their day is going to include.

Relationship skills should be modeled by adults for children. Babies should be approached thoughtfully, calmly, quietly, and with respect. Greeting the child and everyone by name, using gracious terms like please and thank you, and asking about them personally, displays adult skills and cultural norms for the child to expect and follow.

Young children appreciate opportunities to make decisions and thrive with positive feedback about their *responsible decision-making* choices. Spaces and drawers for little ones should be established throughout the home. For example, a low kitchen drawer can store all of the child's sippy cups, plates, baby food, and snacks so that they have the opportunity every day to go to their drawer and exhibit responsible decision-making by selecting their choices. Likewise, laundry baskets may be filled with toys, low bookshelves may be where they can find their storybooks in a comfortable corner, and play-yard spaces may be where they safely listen to music and play independently. Even very young children appreciate and are capable of handling appropriate choices.

Preschool: Three to Five Years of Age

Preschool-age children consistently learn new skills and can develop lifelong skills at this young age. Chapter 4 highlighted three diverse learners and specific activities that benefit their learning and development of social emotional skills. Below are some activities that foster skills in the following areas.

Self-Awareness Activities

- ♦ Creating language and opportunities around identifying emotions. Using various emojis or faces that demonstrate emotions provides children the opportunity to identify the emotion.

- ◆ Encouraging and practicing self-talk when they are feeling a certain way helps provide them with an outlet to help their regulation.
- ◆ Creating role-playing scenarios where students act out or observe others in situations to talk through how they should handle the situation.
- ◆ Building empathy through the use of role-playing and/or with the use of a stuffed animal, doll, or toy. Allowing adults, others, and the children to demonstrate the skills needed within various scenarios.

◆ Involvement with activities to develop critical thinking skills. This can be through various games or solving puzzles or problems. Discussions to develop and identify these skills help build awareness and use. Active modeling of the thinking process is important as well.

◆ Using creative thinking skills to create a new product, picture, or game while only being able to use certain items. Free choice with open-ended activities such as block building or dramatic play are ideas to benefit this area.

Social Awareness Activities

- ◆ Establishing child-focused goals during activity time, such as completing one puzzle before moving to a different center, writing a certain number of items, or using an amount of time with a timer.
- ◆ Developing clear routines so that the child understands the expectations for each day and activity period. This may include singing the clean up song, having a bell when it's clean up time, seeing the schedule for the day or time, or other elements.
- ◆ Using and clarifying transitional expectations for moving between activities. This can be the inclusion of a five-minute warning before moving to the next activity, utilizing a clear schedule with a routine established, or providing verbal or nonverbal cues about transitions. These cues help children self-regulate during the transition.

Conclusion ◆ 97

- ◆ Open-ended activities that require creativity. Including the creation of projects, art activities, participating with sensory tables, blocks, dramatic play, and imaginary play.
- ◆ Role-playing games are beneficial for children to learn verbal and nonverbal communication skills. Acting out various scenarios with other children, props, and/or toys helps young children navigate communication skills and elements.

Relationship Skills Activities
- ◆ As children navigate various settings with new adults and peers, it is critical that they feel safe in their environment. Allowing children to bring a special toy from home helps create safety within the new environment.
- ◆ Impulse control can be challenging as young children begin to navigate new spaces with peers. Using timers reinforces the skill of waiting before accessing a toy, moving on to a new activity, or letting someone else have the toy.
- ◆ Providing children the opportunity for free play both inside and outside. Unstructured play time is important for children to develop relationships, regulation skills, problem solving strategies, and task persistence.
- ◆ Providing modeling for children to use a growth mindset allows the opportunity for preschool children to see the language used. "Yes, and…" strategy can be powerful to develop the positive growth mindset instead of a fixed mindset.

School Age: Six to Eight Years of Age

School-age children have many unique needs in the cognitive, affective, and psychomotor domains. Children start attending school and have a wide variety of different levels due to their language acquisition, access to early education, interactions with books and toys, and access to health and nutrition, among several factors. As discussed in Chapter 5, there are many ways to address

98 ◆ Conclusion

the various needs of school-age children. The following highlight many ways to address the differing social and emotional needs.

Self-Awareness and Self-Management Activities
- ◆ Understanding and identifying one's emotions.
  - ◆ Using bibliotherapy to help children talk through their feelings and identify their feelings.
- ◆ Recognizing strengths.
  - ◆ Creating opportunities to develop specific skills (academic or talent-based such as art or music).
  - ◆ Identifying themselves as an expert in that area to work in groups
  - ◆ Providing high-level academic challenge in terms of skill practice, enrichment, and/or above grade-level tasks.
  - ◆ Encouraging students to self-advocate for their needs in specific areas through the use of mentoring, modeling, and practicing the skill. Bibliotherapy can also be used to reinforce the purpose behind advocating for their needs.
  - ◆ Developing individual goals within and around learning. Utilizing tools to encourage specific goals.
  - ◆ Introducing the "power of yet" strategy whereby students are unable to perform a specific skill and they use the wording "I don't know it yet" instead of "I don't know it."

Social Awareness Activities
- ◆ Creating opportunities where students need to use mental flexibility with how they work through or solve problems. This can be specifically with an open-ended problem, where they are provided a challenge that needs to be solved but they cannot utilize a certain item, or a range of other open-ended problem solving challenges.
- ◆ Project-Based Learning in the classroom. Children identify a real-world project that needs to be completed, requiring the acquisition of new knowledge, development of new skills, and the creation of a project for display.

Conclusion ◆ 99

- ◆ Problem-Based Learning focuses on the aspects of a problem that must be solved. Present a real-world problem that children solve with the use of new knowledge and skills.
- ◆ Range of opportunities for students to participate in group work with pairs, trios, and groups of four to six providing children with the structure and skills to work with a multitude of different personalities, strengths, and challenges.
- ◆ Providing opportunities to use role-play of various scenarios in which children model various challenges that are encountered.

Relationship Skills Activities

- ◆ Create opportunities for children to become experts in specific content or skills and then "teach" other classmates how to complete the skill. Builds leadership skills. (This is different than having the advanced learners teach a skill to other students because they have mastered the skill – the goal of this type of activity is to develop the leadership skills not the content skill).
- ◆ Practice active communication and listening skills. Playing games such as telephone and charades helps children try various forms of communication.
- ◆ Using bibliotherapy as a natural part of the classroom and everyday "read aloud" literacy activities which incorporate social emotional content. Helping children identify with the challenges of the characters and various scenarios and apply them to situations that are similar to them.
- ◆ Providing a range of interest-based clubs encourages students to try a range of different activities and clubs based on interest or on elements that have not been tried previously.
- ◆ Help children identify role models through the use of books including both picture and chapter books. Find a diverse group of individuals and biographies to read about or watch videos and identify traits for each person.

Summary

The early childhood years include children from birth to eight years of age. Across this age range there are a variety of different developmental stages and skills among advanced children. While research has created these stages and skills, no two children are the same and they acquire skills differently and move through the stages at different rates. It is important that adults recognize the specific skills and needs of the child and provide opportunities which are appropriate to their level cognitively, physically, and socially and emotionally. By increasing awareness among families and educators about the psychosocial development of young children and the purposeful use of mindful social emotional learning activities that are differentiated for the needs of advanced children, it is our hope that children will build their emotional self-understanding, thinking skills, confidence, self-esteem, self-advocacy, and positive relationships through a variety of healthy experiences. The social and emotional well-being of young children in early childhood is critical to help them grow and develop into mentally healthy adults.

Appendix A

Book and Article Resources

Early Childhood

Connell, G., McCarthy, C., & Pirie, W. (2016). *Move, play, and learn with smart steps: Sequenced activities to build the body and the brain (birth to age 7)*. Free Spirit Publishing.

>This book focuses on creating an environment for movement in order to help children learn. There are specific lessons, guidelines, and resources for classroom teachers.

Connell, G., & McCarthy, C. (2013). *A moving child is a learning child: How the body teaches the brain to think (birth to age 7)*. Free Spirit Publishing.

>This is a hands-on resource that links brain activity, motor and sensory development, movement, and early learning. There are activities that are geared towards a presented and discussed Kinetic Scale.

Gadzikowski, A. (2013). *Challenging exceptionally bright children in early childhood classrooms*. Redleaf Press.

>This book provides strategies and understanding for young gifted children. There are three sections of focus within the book, differentiation, conversation, and connection. Strategies and guidance are provided in each of these focus areas to meet the needs of young gifted learners in various classroom settings.

Heidemann, S., Menninga, B., & Chang, C. (2020). *Intentional teaching in early childhood: Ignite your passion for learning and improve outcomes for young children*. Free Spirit Publishing.

>This is designed for teachers to engage in their practice and identify the research-based practices for growth. Specifically this book focuses on professional development for teachers.

Hertzog, N. B. & Gadzikowski, A. (2017). *Early childhood gifted education: Fostering talent development (NAGC select series)*. National Association for Gifted Children.

This book provides an overview on characteristics of young gifted learners. The focus is on nurturing talents from a young age and recognizing the types of curricular approaches and models that will work best for the young children.

Hertzog, N. B. (2008). *Ready for preschool: Prepare your child for happiness and success at school.* Prufrock Press.

The focus of this book is to help parents make decisions that will positively impact a child's growth that ultimately impacts school success. There are several chapters that focus on activities to do with your child, and the chapter on social and emotional competencies is a balance between activities and strategies with resources to help implement the strategies.

Olszewski-Kubilius, P., Limburg-Weber, L., & Pfeiffer, S. (Eds.). (2003). *Early gifts: Recognizing and nurturing children's talents.* Prufrock Press.

The focus of this book is how to develop and foster talent in various domain areas such as science, language, music, dramatic arts, math, visual arts, and athletic talents; the social emotional aspect and support is built into the chapters. The last chapter addresses the psychological considerations with four main principles introduced and explained.

Salcedo, M. (2018). *Uncover the roots of challenging behavior: Create responsive environments where young children thrive.* Free Spirit Publishing.

Encourages teachers to analyze their classroom routines, elements, and responses to children. The focus is to develop a strong environment that meets the needs of children thus reducing behavioral challenges in the classroom.

Smutny, J. F., Walker, S. Y., & Honeck, E. I. (2016). *Teaching gifted children in today's preschool and primary classrooms: Identifying, nurturing, and challenging children ages 4–9.* Free Spirit Publishing.

This book focuses specifically on curricular implementation and ideas for young gifted learners. The social emotional aspects of children are woven into the various aspects of the curriculum with one chapter devoted specifically to understanding and meeting the social and emotional needs of children. Specific examples and templates for strategies and ideas are included in the book.

Gifted Characteristics and Gifted Education

Castellano, J. A., & Chandler K. L. (Eds.). (2022). *Identifying and serving diverse gifted learners: Meeting the needs of special populations in gifted education.* Routledge.

This book focuses on equity in gifted education providing resources and information across racial, cultural, and gender diversity. There is a combination of personal narratives, data, research, and tools to help support gifted learners.

DuBois, M. P., & Greene, R. M. (2021). *Supporting gifted ELLs in the Latinx community: Practical strategies, K-12.* Routledge.

This book serves as a guide to help English language learners from the Latinx community in the classroom. There is information on engaging families and communities, practical strategies for culturally responsive assessments, identification, and programming.

Fertig, C. (2021). *Raising a gifted child: A parenting success handbook.* Routledge.

This book offers a large menu of strategies, resources, organizations, tips, and suggestions for parents to find optimal learning opportunities for their kids. The focus is empowering parents by giving them the tools needed to ensure that their gifted kids are happy and successful both in and out of school.

Galbraith, J., & Desile, J. (2015). *When gifted kids don't have all the answers: How to meet their social and emotional needs.* Free Spirit.

This book offers practical suggestions for addressing the social and emotional needs of gifted students. There are case studies and real examples of how to help gifted underachievers, perfectionists, and twice-exceptional students as well as suggestions for creating a safe learning environment.

Inman, T. F., & Kirchner, J. (2016). *Parenting gifted children 101.* Routledge.

This book is to help parents maximize their child's educational experiences utilizing research-based strategies. Along with strategies, there is information about myths and characteristics of giftedness as well as the how and why of advocacy.

Lawson Davis, J. (2022). *Bright, talented, & black: A guide for families of black gifted learners*. Gifted Unlimited.

This book focuses specifically on Black gifted students with real-life examples about how talent has been overlooked and how to support advanced diverse students. Strategies and resources are provided to use in the classroom, with families, and to advocate for students.

Nilles, K., Jolly, J. L., Inman, T. F., & Smutny, J. F. (Eds.). (2021). *Success strategies for parenting gifted kids: Expert advice from the national association for gifted children*. Routledge.

This book includes collated and updated published articles from the National Association for Gifted Children's parenting publication "Parenting for High Potential." The book is divided into eight parts around various gifted education topics. Part II is focused on Early Childhood and Part III is specific to Social Emotional Learning.

Webb, J. T., Gore, J. L., & Amend, E. R. (2007). *A parent's guide to gifted children*. Great Potential Press.

Practical guidance and resources are provided by three professionals with gifted children and families. The writers share insight into their work as psychologists and educators working with families and supporting students throughout many years.

Social Emotional Characteristics and Learning

Bodrova, E., & Leong, D. J. (2008). Developing self-regulation in kindergarten. *Young Children, 63*(2), 56–58.

This article is written specifically with classroom teachers in mind and includes strategies for use in a kindergarten classroom. Self-regulation is the topic and includes how to address the various skills within self-regulation.

Delisle, J. (2018). *Understanding your gifted child from the inside out: A guide to the social and emotional lives of gifted kids*. Routledge.

The author shares real life stories about the lives of gifted children and how they and their parents recognize and enjoy the many intellectual talents and social and emotional insights they possess.

Fonseca, C. (2021). *Emotional intensity in gifted students: Helping kids cope with explosive feelings*. Routledge.

While not specifically for early childhood, this book shares information and practical strategies when working with children and their behaviors. This is designed for both parents and educators covering a range of strategies to help children positively change their behavior.

Fonseca, C. (2020). *Healing the heart: Helping your child thrive after trauma*. Routledge.

The author focuses on various types of trauma as well as providing research related to the brain and trauma. There are handouts to guide children and families through various strategies.

Giroux, L. N. (2022). *Create an emotion-rich classroom: Helping young children build their social emotional skills*. Free Spirit Publishing.

The author provides early childhood educators with resources and strategies to develop the emotional literacy of the young children in their classrooms. Handouts, checklists, and guides support teachers and families.

Hébert, T. P. (2021). *Understanding the social and emotional lives of gifted students*. Routledge.

The author introduces various lived experiences of gifted students, social and emotional characteristics and behaviors, as well as a focus on identity development. This book delves into various social and emotional strategies to utilize with specific challenges.

Kapustka, K., & Bright, S. (2022). *Integrating social and emotional learning with content: Using picture books for differentiated teaching in K-3 classrooms*. Routledge.

This book is designed to use picture books with children in the early primary classrooms. The lessons and selections help children make meaningful connections to academic skills, social and emotional skills, as well as lived experiences.

Kircher-Morris, E. (2022). *Raising twice-exceptional children: A handbook for parents of neurodivergent gifted kids*. Routledge.

This book is designed to help understand gifted identification and the diagnosis of being neurodivergent including dyslexia,

106 ◆ Appendix A

ADHD, Autism, and others. Strategies include meeting social and emotional needs, self-regulation, goal setting, and self-advocacy.

Missett, T. (2014). *The social and emotional characteristics of gifted students (NAGC select series)*. National Association for Gifted Children.

The Select Series is a quick read providing general information and strategies to the reader. This book introduces and discusses social emotional characteristics as well as some strategies to help gifted students.

Neihart, M. (2021). *The social and emotional development of gifted children: What do we know?* Routledge.

This book summarizes research in the area of social and emotional development of gifted children. Each chapter provides a description of the area as well as practical applications of strategies to assist with the social and emotional needs of children.

Zucker, B. (2016). *Anxiety-free kids: An interactive guide for parents and children* (2nd ed.). Routledge.

This book shares strategies for parents that help children become happy and worry-free. Methods and strategies to help relieve a child's excessive anxieties and phobias and tools for fostering family interactions are also included.

Identification Resources for Young Children

Identification of gifted children should include multiple measures and both qualitative and quantitative measures. It is important to recognize that a high score on one of these measures is not enough to be identified as gifted but rather provides information on programming for the student. Similarly, a low score should not exclude a child from participation in higher-level or gifted programming. The list below is a *sampling* of observational rating scales, ability assessments, and intelligence measures.

Cognitive Abilities Test (CogAT)

The CogAT is designed for students K–12 and has separate measures of Verbal, Quantitative, and Nonverbal reasoning. This is a group administered assessment and can use national or local norms.

Frasier Talent Assessment Profile (F-Tap)

The F-Tap is a multidimensional talent identification and educational development system that utilizes a variety of data. There are ten TABS (traits, aptitudes, and behaviors) that students are evaluated on by individuals in different contexts. These TABS include motivation, interests, communication skills, problem solving ability, memory, inquiry, insight, reasoning, imagination/creativity, and humor. This assessment is designed specifically for Culturally Linguistically Diverse Learners.

Gifted Evaluation Scale (GES)

This observational scale is designed for students K–12 and is a nationally normed assessment. The scale measures across several categories of giftedness including intellectual, creativity, specific academic aptitude, leadership ability, and performing and visual arts with an optional category on motivation.

Gifted Rating Scale (GRS)

The GRS has two versions, the GRS-P for preschool and kindergarten students and the GRS-S for children in grades first to eighth grade. This rating scale has up to six categories on which the rater evaluates the child's ability including intellectual ability, academic ability, creativity, artistic talent, motivation, and for the GRS-S also leadership ability. This is a nationally normed rating scale.

Naglieri Nonverbal Ability Test® Third Edition (NNAT®3)

This is a nonverbal small group administered measure of general ability for students in kindergarten through grade 12. This is a nationally normed assessment and can use local norms.

Scales for Identifying Gifted Students (SIGS)

SIGS has both a school rating form and a home rating form. The questions on the scale are across multiple categories such as general intellectual ability, language arts, mathematics, science, social studies, creativity, and leadership. This is a nationally normed rating scale.

The HOPE Teacher Rating Scale

This is a rating scale based on teacher observations to focus on specific components of giftedness. This is designed with culturally, economically, and linguistically diverse students in mind. The ratings include components of giftedness in the academic and social/affective domains. This rating scale can be locally normed.

U-STARS~PLUS: Using Science, Talents, and Abilities to Recognize Students ~ Promoting Learning for Under-Represented Students

This observation tool is designed to engage teachers to make intentional and purposeful observations so that those observations can be used to provide more effective instruction and focus on individual strengths.

Weschler Intelligence Scale for Children (WISC)

The Weschler Intelligence Scale for Children is an individual intelligence test that scores children ages six to 16 in verbal comprehension, visual spatial, working memory, fluid reasoning, and processing speed. This assessment must be administered by a licensed psychologist. The Weschler Preschool and Primary Scale of Intelligence (WPPSI) is designed for children 2.6 to seven years old.

Appendix B
Social and Emotional Learning Curriculum Resources

Curriculum Resources

The curriculum resources in this section include materials that have lessons, units, and frameworks to utilize with students. There are many SEL curriculums and lessons built around specific skills. This list is a sampling of some of the materials that the authors have found helpful with young gifted children.

Hannenfent, M. (2007). *Learning to be a durable person: Social and emotional activities and teacher guide (grades K-5)*. Routledge.
> This book is designed for gifted learners and has activities related to social emotional skills that can be utilized in grade K–5. Units include topics of creativity, goal setting, careers, teasing, stress, anger, and making friends.

Hess, M. (2021). *Social & emotional curriculum for gifted students grade 3: Project-based learning lessons that build critical thinking, emotional intelligence, and social skills*. Routledge.
> While the lessons are geared towards third-grade students, many activities can be scaffolded to younger learners. Topics that are included are self-understanding, individuality, growth mindset, identity, empathy, and compassion.

Petersen, K. S. (2012). *Activities for building character and social-emotional learning grades PreK-K*. Free Spirit Publishing.
> The lessons designed in the early childhood teacher resource are focused on teaching young children positive life skills through daily practice. The lessons and activities focus on guiding students to be curious, active, and imaginative.

110 ◆ Appendix B

Petersen, K. S. (2012). *Activities for building character and social-emotional learning grades 1–2*. Free Spirit Publishing.

Lessons are not specifically for gifted students; however the lessons focus on respect and caring, problem behaviors, solving problems, and focus on the whole child. There are literature connections to help teachers build on lessons.

Random Acts of Kindness Foundation. https://www.randomactso fkindness.org/.

The website has free K–8 lessons, high school lessons, mini-lessons for distance learning, training materials for teachers, and suggestions for school to home connections. There are many resources in addition to the school materials accessible via the website.

Stambaugh, T., & VanTassel-Baska, J. (2021). *Affective Jacob's Ladder reading comprehension program: Social-emotional intelligence grade 2*. Routledge.

This series of affective lessons build on a model of "ladders" focusing on emotional intelligence, coping with adversity and challenge, risk taking, developing identity, developing empathy, stress management, achievement motivation, and developing talent and excellence. There are specific grade-level reading level connections to build skills in one of the above areas.

Stambaugh, T., & VanTassel-Baska, J. (2021). *Affective Jacob's Ladder reading comprehension program: Social-emotional intelligence grade 3*. Routledge.

This series of affective lessons build on a model of "ladders" focusing on emotional intelligence, coping with adversity and challenge, risk taking, developing identity, developing empathy, stress management, achievement motivation, and developing talent and excellence. There are specific grade-level reading level connections to build skills in one of the above areas.

Picture Books for Bibliotherapy

Bibliotherapy uses books to help children connect to characters that are addressing social and emotional challenges. There are many books available depending on what skills are the focus. The following books

Appendix B ◆ 111

are all picture books and some include an adult section for using the book. While this is a *small sampling* of books available, we recommend investigating various publishers and book collections such as the ones available on the Free Spirit Publishing's website https://www.freespirit.com/. Books and book series are available for various ages of children as young as babies and toddlers.

Anderson, S. (2015). *Penelope perfect: A tale of perfectionism gone wild*. Free Spirit Publishing.
>This book helps the reader understand and develop strategies to address when things don't go as planned. Penelope is a fun and relatable character.

Britain, L., & Rivera, M. (2019). *I'm happy-sad today: Making sense of mixed-together feelings*. Free Spirit Publishing.
>This book presents feelings and helps children understand that more than one emotion can be felt at the same time. The combination of emotions is presented as well as some fun word play.

Byers, G. (2018). *I am enough*. Balzer + Bray.
>Written as an ode, the focus is to help children understand to respect each other, love themself, and be kind to others.

Hertzog, N., Honeck, E., & Dullaghan, B. (2015). *Around my house! (smart start series, book 1)*. Prufrock Press.
>The Smart Start series guides families and parents in questioning strategies for creative thinking, critical thinking, and mathematical thinking question stems using the images in the book. Images in this book show children in settings around the house: in the kitchen, the playroom, the bedroom, the garage, and more.

Hertzog, N., Honeck, E., & Dullaghan, B. (2015). *Let's go to the market! (smart start series, book 3)*. Prufrock Press.
>The Smart Start series guides families and parents in questioning strategies for creative thinking, critical thinking, and mathematical thinking question stems using the images in the book. Images in this book show children in various types of markets across the globe.

Hertzog, N., Honeck, E., & Dullaghan, B. (2015). *Let's play! (smart start series, book 2)*. Prufrock Press.

112 ◆ Appendix B

The Smart Start series guides families and parents in questioning strategies for creative thinking, critical thinking, and mathematical thinking question stems using the images in the book. Images in this book show children in playing in various settings inside and outside of the house.

Mental Health board book collection by Verdick from Free Spirit Publishing.
https://www.freespirit.com/mental-health-board-book-collection.
This series includes books with a focus on easing worries and helping toddlers calm down and feel valued. Sample titles in this series include *I Feel, I Belong*, *Worries Are Not Forever*, *Calm-Down Timer*, and *Manners Time*.

Kids Can Cope series by Hasson & Jennings from Free Spirit Publishing.
https://www.freespirit.com/series/kids-can-cope.
This series includes books with various characters facing a variety of challenges. Topics include coping with feelings related to disappointment, fear, jealousy, fear, anxiety, shyness, frustration, and teasing. Sample titles include *Take Charge of Anger*, *Put Your Worries Away*, *Step Back from Frustration*, *Let Go of Jealousy*, and *Face Your Fears*.

Learning to Get Along series by Meiners & Johnson from Free Spirit Publishing. https://www.freespirit.com/series/learning-to-get-along/.
This series includes books to help children learn and practice social skills. Topics include politeness, kindness, safety, valuing others, being polite, including others, anger, following rules, listening, sharing, and respect. Some sample titles include *Share and Take Turns*, *Respect and Take Care of Things*, *Listen and Learn*, *Be Polite and Kind*, and *Accept and Value Each Person*.

Good Habits with Coco and Tula book series by Geis from Windmill Books.
This series focuses upon Coco demonstrating good habits. For example, in *Let's Help*, Coco demonstrates helpfulness by cleaning his room, watering the plants, setting the table, and putting the clothes in the hamper. Some sample titles include *Let's Wash Up!*, *Let's Get Well!*, *Let's Go to Sleep!*, and *Let's Help!*

Gershator, P. (2012). *Time for a hug*. Sterling Children's Books.

> Morning, noon, or night – anytime is a great time for a hug! This book demonstrates the ease and fun of giving and receiving hugs throughout the day.

Martin, M. and Lehman, C. (2017). *Tessie Tames her tongue: A book about learning when to talk and when to listen*. Free Spirit Publishing.

> This book focuses on a child that has difficulty listening. As Tessie learns the importance of listening, the reader learns different strategies to help.

Nyong'o, L. (2019). *Sulwe*. Penguin Publishing.

> This book focuses on the character Sulwe and finding the beauty in her skin color. The goal is to help children find their own unique beauty.

Our Emotions and Behavior series by Graves, Carletti, & Guicciardini from Free Spirit Publishing. https://www.freespirit.com/series/our-emotions-and-behavior/.

> This series includes 12 books focusing on topics such as feeling worried, telling the truth, kindness, rules, patience, respect, being brave, sharing being a good sport, feeling sad, afraid, and angry. A sampling of the titles include *I Want to Win*, *No Fair*, *I Don't Want to Share*, *I Hate Everything*, and *Take a Deep Breath*.

How Monsters Wish to Feel and other picture books Seven Storybook Set by Juliette Ttofa. https://www.routledge.com/How-Monsters-Wish-to-Feel-and-other-picture-books-Seven-Storybooks-Set/Ttofa/p/book/9781138556478.

> This is a series of seven therapeutic story books. Each book has an accompanying guide that can be purchased as a companion piece. Titles include *How Monsters Wish to Feel: A Story about Emotional Resilience*, *The Boat Star: A Story about Loss*, *The Boy Who Longed to Look at the Sun: A Story about Self-Care*, *The Day the Sky Fell In: A Story about Finding your Element*, *The Girl Who Collected Her Own Echo: A Story about Friendship*, *The Hot and Bothered Air Balloon: A Story about Feeling Stressed*, and *The Tale of Two Fishes: A Story about Resilient Thinking*.

Appendix C

Organizational Resources

Organizational Resources

Collaborative for Academic, Social, and Emotional Learning (CASEL) – https://casel.org/

CASEL created a framework for social and emotional learning that has a strong equity focus by developing and supporting school, family, and community relationships. The organization focuses strongly on including SEL content across all curriculum and instruction and for all grade levels. The site has research and resources for classrooms, schools, districts, families, and community members.

Council for Exceptional Children – The Association for the Gifted (CEC-TAG) – https://cectag.com/

CEC-TAG is a special interest division of the larger organization of Council for Exceptional Children. CEC ensures that there is a voice in educational legislation for children with exceptionalities as well as developing initiatives for gifted education teacher training, improving gifted education practice, and twice exceptionalities.

National Association for the Education of Young Children (NAEYC) – www.naeyc.org

NAEYC focuses specifically on early childhood development. The NAEYC has position papers that focus on various aspects of young children's health, development, care, and education. This organization has member features that include publications, online content, seminar discounts, and more. There are also state associations for this organization that offer some of the same features.

National Association of Gifted Children (NAGC) – www.nagc.org

NAGC is the largest association in the United States focusing on giftedness. There are many free resources on the website and there are many member-related features such as various Network newsletters (Social and Emotional Development and Early Childhood, among others) and publications such as *Gifted Child Today*, *Parenting for High Potential*, *Teaching for High Potential*, and *Gifted Child Quarterly*. There are often state associations that have similar features on a local level.

P21 Partnership for 21st Century Learning A Network of Battelle for Kids – www.battelleforkids.org/networks/p21/frameworks-resources

The Frameworks for 21st Century Learning were created with input from teachers, education experts, and business leaders. The frameworks identify the skills and learner outcomes for children as young as toddlers. The site has a learning hub with research, blogs, videos, and schools that successfully implement the frameworks.

Supporting Emotional Needs of the Gifted (SENG) – www.sengifted.org

SENG has online articles that address varying topics related to the social emotional needs of gifted children. The website also sponsors SENGinars (webinars on various topics), a blog, a news-letter, and many other features.

Appendix D

Definitions of Relevant Terminology

Professionals, such as early childhood educators, use words and terminology specific to their field.Below is a glossary of some commonly used early childhood terms. Readers may also refer to the National Association for the Education of Young Children (NAEYC), the world's largest organization for early childhood educators, for more information.

Glossary

Affective Development is the area of a child's growth that includes personality, emotions, making and changing friends, social skills, and the child's perception of his/her self.

Assessment, or Child Assessment refers to information (usually from multiple sources) that is collected, examined, and interpreted to make an appraisal of the child or judgment about the child's development, abilities, or needs.

Asynchronous Development is the uneven development in childhood across the areas of cognition, socialization, emotions, and physical growth.

Attachment is a psychological bond between adult and child. It is believed that secure bonding leads to psychological well-being and resistance to ordinary as well as extreme stress experienced throughout a lifetime. Key signs of attachment between a child and an adult are:

1. The child looks at their caretaker as the adult moves away from the child.
2. The child moves toward their caretaker upon return after separation.
3. The child goes to their caretaker when upset, may cling, and finds personal comfort in being together.

Appendix D ◆ 117

4. When their caretaker is present, the child feels safe and begins to gain confidence to look around, explore, and leave to play with other children or to explore objects and their environment.

Children who have secure attachment relationships with their teachers or day carers will accept comfort from them when the child is upset, as well as easily follow their directions, approach their teacher for hugs, and be playful with their teacher.

Autism is a developmental disorder that affects a child's ability to communicate and interact with others. For reasons that are not clear, the disease is three to four times more common in boys than it is in girls. Autism often appears in early childhood, usually before a child is three years of age. In general, autism affects three areas of a child's development: language, social interaction, and behavior. Some children may show symptoms of autism in early infancy. Others develop normally for the first several months or years of life, with symptoms appearing later. Most children with autism have significant symptoms by the time they reach their third birthday (Jensen, 2013).

Best Practices is a term used to denote the ways of delivering services that have been found through research or experience as the "best" ways to achieve desired outcomes.

Center-Based Child Care Programs are licensed or otherwise authorized to provide childcare services in a non-residential setting.

Child Development is the process by which a child acquires skills in the areas of social, emotional, intellectual, speech and language, and physical development, including fine and gross motor skills. Developmental stages refer to the expected, sequential order of acquiring skills that children typically go through. For example, most children crawl before they walk, or use their fingers to feed themselves before they use utensils.

Cognitive Development is also known as intellectual development. The word "cognitive" refers to the intellectual mind and how it works, how knowledge is learned, and the way knowledge is used.

Development is physical growth and other changes that occur from conception and across the life span. It's thought by theorists that individuals develop as a result of natural maturation or by learning in the environment or as a result of both maturation and learning.

Developmental Assessment is the measurement of a child's cognitive, language, knowledge, and psychomotor skills in order to evaluate development in comparison to children of the same chronological age.

Developmental Domains is a term used to describe areas of a child's development, including "gross motor development" (large muscle movement and control); "fine motor development" (hand and finger skills, and hand-eye coordination); speech and language/communication; the child's relationship to toys and other objects, to people, and to the larger world around them; and the child's emotions and feeling states, coping behavior, and self-help skills.

Developmental Milestone can be a memorable accomplishment on the part of a baby or young child; for example, rolling over, sitting up without support, crawling, pointing to get an adult's attention, or walking.

Developmentally Appropriate is a way of describing practices that are adapted to match the age, characteristics, and developmental progress of a specific age group of children.

Developmentally Appropriate Practice (DAP) is a concept of classroom practice that reflects knowledge of child development and an understanding of the unique personality, learning style, and family background of each child. DAP activities are not too difficult or too easy, but just right. These practices are defined by the National Association for the Education of Young Children (NAEYC).

Differentiation is recognizing individual differences and trying to find institutional strategies which take account of them for enhanced learning experiences and talent development.

Early Entrance, Kindergarten is the strategy used to make educational accommodations for young children with advanced cognitive abilities.

Early Intervention refers to a range of services designed to enhance the development of children with disabilities or at risk of developmental delay. Early intervention services under public supervision generally must be given by qualified personnel and require the development of an individualized family service plan.

Early Learning Programs benefit children with a strong foundation in many different areas and provide the opportunity to develop self-awareness as capable learners.

Extended Day Program is a term that refers to programs for school-age children and provides supervision, academic enrichment, and recreation for children of working parents after school hours end.

Family Child Care refers to child care provided for a group of children in a home setting. Most states have regulatory guidelines for family child care homes if they serve a number of children or families over a specified threshold or if they operate more than a specified number of hours each month.

Family Literacy refers to literacy for all family members. Family literacy programs frequently combine adult literacy, preschool/school-age education, and parenting education.

Free Play is an unhurried time for children to choose their own play activities, with a minimum of adult direction. Providers may observe, intervene, or join the play, as needed. Free play may be indoors or outdoors.

Giftedness, federal definition, "the term gifted and talented means students, children, or youth who give evidence of high achievement capability in such areas as intellectual, creative, artistic, or leadership capacity, or in specific academic fields, and who need services or activities not ordinarily provided by the school in order to fully develop those capabilities" (Marland Report to Congress, 1972).

Guidance encourages appropriate child behavior by helping young children understand that they can learn from the mistakes made by themselves or by others in an encouraging setting that promotes self-control, teaches responsibility, and helps children make thoughtful choices. Guidance is not punishing children for making mistakes; it is helping children to learn from their mistakes. Guidance is not disciplining children for having problems they cannot solve, but assisting children to learn to solve their problems. Friendly humor is important in good guidance as well as three considerations:

1. When using guidance, adults are firm when needed, but firm and friendly, not firm and harsh.
2. Teachers who use guidance do well to think of a child's age in terms of months rather than years. They understand that young children are just beginning to learn difficult life skills that may take a lifetime to master.
3. A partnership between the teacher, the child, and the family is necessary for guidance to be effective.

Observation is a process used by early childhood educators to watch, listen to, and record children's actions, facial expressions, body language, sounds, words, and gestures. Educators use the information collected through observations for different purposes. Observation helps educators get to know children so that they can build positive relationships with them, identify a child's preferred playmates, what the child knows about a topic, or understand what and how a child is thinking, feeling, and learning and plan ways to support and enhance the child's development of skills in all domains. To be most useful, observations can be recorded in writing, in digital format, through photographs, or through use of multiple strategies. When examined over time, observation recordings can document a child's progress.

Oral Language includes speaking and listening. For preschoolers, it involves understanding and using a growing vocabulary. Development of oral language skills begins in infancy as children listen to adults and older siblings talk to each other and to them. While oral language develops naturally, the more a child hears and is engaged in conversation, the greater his or her language skills will be.

A **Portfolio** includes thoughtfully collected examples of an individual child's work along with other items, such as photos and observation notes, to document the child's activities over time. Teachers use portfolios for ongoing planning and assessment of the child's learning and as a tool for demonstrating to the child, family, and others the child's efforts, progress, and achievements in general and in relation to specific early learning standards. A less formal portfolio is a scrapbook of milestones that is kept throughout childhood.

A **Print-Rich Preschool Environment** offers children many different materials for reading and writing and the time and opportunities to use them for a wide variety of authentic, everyday purposes. Such learning environments include books, magazines, and other forms of print; use signs and labels to communicate information; and offer paper and writing tools throughout the room. Children can look at books alone or with a friend, sign their names on the daily attendance chart, write cards and letters, record observations, and incorporate reading and writing in their play.

A **Reflective Teacher** considers what they know about a child or situation, child development theory, and past experiences, then uses new knowledge and insights to plan next steps in teaching and learning. In action, a reflective teacher watches children's play, documents children's conversations, studies notes and photos to learn what is significant, reads professional literature, exchanges information with families, and applies this new information to plan ways to engage a child and encourage learning.

Resilience is the ability to bounce back from traumas, frustrations, and challenges. Resilient children and adults have the ability to figure out strategies to cope with difficulties rather than being overwhelmed by them. Resilient preschoolers tend to be able to do things on their own, but will ask for help when needed. They are optimistic, know their own strengths, have healthy and supportive relationships with peers and family, and take charge of their own learning.

To help preschoolers build resilience, educators can nurture children's beliefs that they are capable and independent.

They can comment on children's efforts as well as noticing their accomplishments. Teachers can help children see challenges and hard effort as normal; build strategies for children to use in difficult situations; and foster a classroom community that supports problem solving through a range of experiences.

Shared Reading is an interactive read-aloud strategy that is similar to what families provide at home, but carried out in early childhood settings. Using oversize books with large print, teachers engage children in the read-aloud process. All the children can see the illustrations and text and possibly feel like the book is being read especially to them. Often teachers introduce children to print concepts through strategies such as pointing out letters and words on the pages of the book, identifying capital letters, and noting that words are written and read from left to right and from the top to the bottom of the page.

Social Development is the pattern or process of change exhibited by individuals resulting from their interaction with other individuals, social institutions, social customs, etc.

Social Promotion, in the education field, is the term that refers to the process of passing students on to the next level or grade based on age or social maturity rather than academic accomplishment.

Socialization refers to the process of how younger family or group members become expert members of the family or group to which they belong.

Thinking Routines typically consist of a series of questions that help children connect past experiences and events with the present, thereby constructing knowledge. Effective teachers use thinking routines to lead children through the steps of critical thinking and help them understand the source of their ideas.Thinking routines allow children to direct and make sense of their own learning. Project Zero, an educational research group at the Graduate School of Education at Harvard University, has developed a set of thinking routines that teachers can use with children, including preschoolers. To read more, visit http://pzweb.harvard.edu.

Zone of Proximal Development is a psychological term that refers to the difference between what a child can do individually and what the child can do with guidance or help from a more expert child or adult.

Bibliography

Child Forum. (2010). *Early childhood jargon and terminology.* http://www.childforum.com/early-childhood-jargon-terminology.html #ixzz2aYPfgNWB.

Jensen, P. (2013). *Early diagnosis can make a big difference in child's ability to manage autism.* Chicago Tribune, March 21, www.chicagotribune.com/lifestyles/ct-xpm-2013-03-21-sns-201303211930-tms-mayoclnctnmc-a20130321-20130321-story.html

Mayo Clinic. (1998–2013). *Mayo Foundation for Medical Education and Research (MFMER).* http://www.mayoclinic.com/health/AboutThisSite/SB00034.

Mayo Clinic Medical Edge Newspaper Column. http://www.mayoclinic.org/medical-edge-newspaper-2013/mar-22a.html.

National Association for the Education of Young Children (NAEYC). *Growing glossary of early childhood terms.* Teaching Young Children. http://www.naeyc.org/tyc/eceglossary.

National Center for Children in Poverty. (2013). *Child care and early education glossary. Child care and early education research connections.* http://www.researchconnections.org/childcare/childcare-glossary.

National Center for Infants, Toddlers, and Families. (2009). *Parenting infants and toddlers today: Young children's social-emotional development: Key findings from a 2009 national parent survey.* www.zerotothree.org/parentsurvey.

Printed in the United States
by Baker & Taylor Publisher Services